About the author—
WALTH┌┌
at sev┌
the
whi┌
the   a.
associa┌
in Zuri┌

THE OLD TESTAMENT
AND THE WORLD

WALTHER ZIMMERLI

THE OLD TESTAMENT
AND THE WORLD

TRANSLATED BY
JOHN J. SCULLION, S.J.

JOHN KNOX PRESS
ATLANTA
1976

Translated from the German
Die Weltlichkeit des Alten Testaments
with permission of
Vandenhoeck & Ruprecht, Göttingen

Published in the United States of America by
John Knox Press, Atlanta, Georgia 1976
and in London, Great Britain by
SPCK 1976

Library of Congress Cataloging in Publication Data

Zimmerli, Walther, 1907-
The Old Testament and the world.

Translation of Die Weltlichkeit des alten Testaments.
Includes bibliographical references and indexes.
1. World in the Bible—Addresses, essays, lectures.
2. Bible. O.T.—Theology—Addresses, essays, lectures.
I. Title.
BS1199.W74Z5513   1976   221.6'6   75-32946
ISBN 0-8042-0139-0

Printed in the United States of America
Atlanta, Georgia

CONTENTS

TRANSLATOR'S NOTE

Versions of texts from the Ancient East follow *Ancient Near Eastern Texts*, ed. J. B. Pritchard, Princeton University Press (1955). The quotation from Plato's *Timaeus* in Chapter 2 follows the version of the Loeb Classical Library.

AUTHOR'S PREFACE
(ABRIDGED)

The following reflections were presented in a series of eleven lectures to those enrolled in all faculties at the University of Göttingen in the summer semester of 1970. The lectures—and this is obvious, especially from the last of the series—were provoked by Rudolph Bultmann's thesis that the biblical proclamation experiences its 'de-sscularization' in the message of the New Testament, and that the Old Testament retains its significance in the Christian Church only by its 'failure'. The lectures are directed at the same time to the more recent question of the relevance of the Old Testament message to the world. Consequently the theological point of departure takes priority over the application to the problems of the moment. The reader is not exempted from the task of translating this into his everyday life.

The reflections are not directed primarily to Old Testament specialists; they aim rather at bringing to a wider circle of readers a particular aspect of the Old Testament attitude to life. There is, then, by and large, no 'specialist discussion' in the narrower sense.

INTRODUCTION:
THE OLD TESTAMENT AND
THE WORLD

The New Testament, the second part of the Christian Bible, gives some sharp warnings about the world: 'Do not set your hearts on the godless world or anything in it. Anyone who loves the world is a stranger to the Father's love' (1 John 2.15). And a little later comes the statement: 'And that world is passing away with all its allurements, but he who does God's will stands for ever more' (2.17). God and the world are set in sharpest contrast to each other. One who listens to God cannot listen to the world. And one who listens to the world loses God. Man is faced with a clear choice: either—or.

The consequence of these verses seems quite clear: Christian faith which is a genuine Christian faith can in no circumstances be 'worldly'. But what does it mean to be 'not worldly'? The 'spiritual' is usually opposed to 'worldly'. Christian faith then must be spiritual, turned away from the world and directed to the world of the spirit, to the heavenly.

This is still the current understanding. One does not have to go far into the history of the Christian Church or into the life of the good Christian today to come up against a firm mistrust of all that is of the world: possession, politics, family, joy in living. And where this has not led to an asceticism which has turned away definitively from the things of the world, it has nevertheless given rise to a secret insecurity in the Christian, to an avowed or perhaps even unavowed attitude of alienation from the transitory and ever unspiritual world.

Now the first part of the Christian Bible, the Old Testament, which comprises no less than three-quarters of the whole Bible, contains a great deal which runs quite contrary to this from-the-world-alienated spirituality, and which is very striking in its

1

extensive involvement in the things and affairs, joys and sorrows, of the world.

Opposition to this worldly part of the Bible began to show itself early. The Gnostic, Marcion, had already excluded it from his Bible in the second century. He saw the demiurge, the creator of the world and the just judge, to whom this book bears witness, as the opponent of the good God who brought the gospel of love in Christ.[1]

The Church at large, which had made very generous accommodation for various currents of asceticism and flight from the world, resorted to other means, in that it went behind the literal meaning of the text and discovered in the spiritual and allegorical meaning many ways of evading the all too worldly declarations. Opposition to the worldly Old Testament has not died down even in our own times. For Bultmann the worth of the Old Testament as promise consists solely in its history of failure, and what is new in the New Testament is its 'de-secularization' of the message.[2] However different in intent is this view from that of Marcion, one cannot nevertheless overlook its profound mistrust of the Old Testament as bound to this world and experienced as un-Christian.

This is the justification of an inquiry, in proper context, into the nature and structure of the attitude of the Old Testament to the world. And so at the conclusion, one will not sidestep the question: what right has this 'worldly book' to a place in the canonical writing of the Christian Church which proclaims the Gospel?

1

ISRAEL AND HER GOD

The Old Testament is the collection of writings which the Christian community received from Israel. This collection developed in three concentric circles around an innermost kernel called the Torah, i.e. Yahweh's 'instruction'.[1] When Israel listens to what was written, she listens to the instruction her God has given her. The attitude to the world which characterizes the Old Testament cannot be understood apart from this instruction which should not be limited to some sort of legalistic prescription devoid of historical setting. The many and varied commandments of the Torah are woven into an account of an historical event, a leading-into and a guiding-through the desert, which is essential to their understanding.

One is led then to inquire into the beginnings of Yahweh's instruction to Israel and to examine the meaning of 'world' in this setting. The beginning can often reveal quite clearly the laws of growth which govern the life of a developing entity.

A consideration of the beginnings of the divine instruction suggests a consideration of the beginnings, of the origins, of which the book of Genesis speaks in its first chapters. Genesis gives an account of the creation of the world and of the order established at the very beginning. One could well suppose that the basic lines of the Old Testament attitude to the world might be recognized here.

We do not meet Israel in these early chapters. She is addressed in a broader context than that of God's own people.[2] We are concerned with the world in its breadth and in its basic outlines. And our customary way of thinking is such that we understand the particular from the general, that we begin with the principles and then judge the particular in the light of the general principles.

Further penetration of the text forbids this procedure, however normal it may be for us. Another approach is necessary. This new approach is suggested not so much by attending to the phenomenon 'world' which certainly occurs in the Genesis stories, as by grasping what the expressions describing God are really saying. It is the realization of the striking way in which the name for God is used that compels us to a different judgement about the focal point of Yahweh's instruction. A few remarks from the standpoint of the history of religions are necessary here.

One of the widely acknowledged conclusions of the critical study of the Pentateuch is that the narrative sections of the five books as we have them today are the result of the interweaving of at least three older written sources.[3] The oldest of these, the Yahwistic source, speaks quite ingenuously of God as Yahweh, and that from the very beginning. Not so the two other sources. The Elohistic source, which also belongs to the pre-exilic period, and however fragmentary its present state of preservation, recognizes that the name Yahweh by which God is addressed in Israel was revealed first to Moses.

Chapter 3 of the book of Exodus narrates in its Elohistic section that Moses had escaped from Egypt as a fugitive and was living in Midian in Arabia.[4] On one occasion while he was guarding the flocks of his father-in-law Jethro at the mountain of God, Horeb, he came across a bush which was in flames but which was not being consumed. God called to him out of this mysterious fire and commissioned him to lead the people of Israel out of Egypt; he had heard their cry as they were in forced labour. Moses replied with a counter-question which surprises the reader: 'If I go to the Israelites and tell them that the god of their forefathers has sent me to them, and they ask me his name, what shall I say?' Yahweh's reply is a word of sovereign refusal, which reveals the majesty of one who does not readily surrender himself in his name. His answer, 'I AM; that is who I am', indicates at the same time that his name is hidden in this sovereign reply: 'Tell them that I AM has sent you to them.' And the riddle of this reply is fully unravelled in a further explanation: 'You must tell the Israelites this, that it is YHWH the God of their forefathers, the God of Abraham, the God of Isaac, the God of Jacob, who has sent you to them. This is my name for ever; this is my title in every generation.' The Hebrew word, *'ehyeh*, 'I AM', which reveals the majesty of him who is ever the sovereign free one, is at the same time the revelation of the name Yahweh, by which Israel with every right acknowledges and invokes her God.

One can hear behind this story the decisive claim: it is only since the time of Moses that Israel knows the God who will guide her on the way as the God who comes to save her from Egypt. The more general title, God of the Fathers, which Albrecht Alt had shown with probability to sum up the belief in God of Israel's forefathers in the period preceding the knowledge of the name of Yahweh,[5] is now replaced by the title, God of Israel, under Yahweh's direct intervention. This important insight of the Elohist is underscored quite impressively by an account from the priestly writings. This latest of the three sources, which is yet to be reconstructed fully, is quite different in its presentation. The dramatic scenery of the burning bush on God's holy mountain has disappeared. God reveals himself to Moses in an episode which is clearly set in Egypt:

> I am the Lord. I appeared to Abraham, Isaac, and Jacob as *El Shaddai* (God Almighty). But I did not let myself be known to them by my name YHWH. Moreover, I made a covenant with them to give them Canaan, the land where they settled for a time as foreigners. And now I have heard the groaning of the Israelites, enslaved by the Egyptians, and I have called my covenant to mind. Say therefore to the Israelites, 'I am the Lord. I will release you from your labours in Egypt. I will rescue you from slavery there. I will redeem you with arm outstretched and with mighty acts of judgement. I will adopt you as my people, and I will become your God. You shall know that I, the Lord, am your God, the God who releases you from your labours in Egypt.' (Exod. 6.2ff.)

We have here another divine title under which the Fathers invoked God. The claim which the priestly writer makes here is quite as unambiguous as that made by the Elohist: Yahweh first revealed his name when he led the people out of Egypt under Moses. The witness of these two sources, which usually go their own way, is impressive. It says all that need be said for the reliability of the memory that the name of Yahweh by which the Old Testament invokes God, and consequently faith in Yahweh as such, has its origin in the time of Moses. It was only in the context of the Exodus that the name took on its quite exclusive meaning for those who were escaping from Egypt. The Yahwistic tradition, though older than the other two, had already absorbed this piece of information.[6]

When we inquire then into the sources of Yahweh's instruction to Israel, we will not begin with the creation stories. We will be proceeding correctly when we take seriously the claims of the two sources already outlined, that the beginnings of the instruction are to be found in the period of the Exodus. This will be the point of departure for our inquiry into the attitude of the Old Testament to the world. Then, and with reference to our findings, we will consider what the early chapters of Genesis have to say.

A further critical definition of the problem, however, must take precedence. In the last years of the nineteenth century Flinders Petrie discovered in the mortuary temple of the Pharaoh Merneptah a stela inscribed with a hymn commemorating a victory which took place about 1230 B.C.[7] A group called 'Israel' is mentioned among the conquered Canaanites, and this at a time when those who had left Egypt were not yet counted among the settled residents of the land. This, and other pieces of evidence, suggests that there was a group 'Israel' already in the land before those who left Egypt made their way there. The twelve tribes of Israel are a development of the period after the land had been occupied. There is much to be said for the view that the report of the assembly at Shechem in Joshua 24 contains a recollection of a ceremony which joined the tribes who were already in the land under the banner of Yahweh. Joshua addresses the tribes gathered together at Shechem:

> Hold the Lord in awe then, and worship him in loyalty and truth. Banish the gods whom your fathers worshipped beside the Euphrates and in Egypt, and worship the Lord. But if it does not please you to worship the Lord, choose here and now whom you will worship: the gods whom your forefathers worshipped beside the Euphrates, or the gods of the Amorites in whose land you are living.
> Joshua then proclaims decisively: But I and my family, we will worship the Lord.

One sees behind the dramatic presentation in these and the preceding verses a call to those tribes who do not yet serve Yahweh to make a definitive commitment to him. The union and establishment of the twelve tribes of Israel could well have had its origin here.[8]

If these surmises are correct, then we should count only the small group that came out of Egypt, the house of Joseph, as the first worshippers of Yahweh. They confessed Yahweh who had delivered them when they groaned under forced labour in Egypt; the others, who were already a group of tribes united under the name of Israel, joined them and their confession, partly forgetting their own religious traditions and partly assimilating them to the confession of Yahweh. The Elohist, who speaks of the worship of the God of the Fathers in the earlier period, and the priestly writer, who calls the one who had been worshipped previously *El Shaddai*, have preserved, each in a different way, a memory of that internal reshaping and assimilation of an ancient belief to belief in Yahweh.

These preliminary observations from the standpoint of the history of religions were necessary. We are now in a position to consider the significance of the early statements of what subsequently became the confession of the faith of the whole of Israel for the question of the attitude of the Old Testament to the world. This confession is reflected quite clearly in the preamble to the Decalogue when the one who appears to the people on God's mountain introduces himself with the words: 'I am Yahweh, your God, who led you out of the land of Egypt, out of the house of slavery' (Exod. 20.2). This confession makes it clear that Israel did not derive her knowledge of God and, of course, the instructions of her God from a general belief in the creation; rather she is conscious that this knowledge is founded on a quite concrete encounter in the course of her history. It is not the general which stands at the beginning; rather it is the concrete encounter. Israel knows her God from the experience of being saved. It was there that she discovered the historical instruction of her God. In this light is also found what is more general.

It is to be noted that there follows immediately in the Decalogue the demand: 'You shall have no other gods beside me.' There are many questions here which are still unresolved—when and how was this old exclusive demand joined to the confession of the God who saved them out of Egypt; and when was the first commandment of the Decalogue as we have it today formulated? R. Knierim has expressed the opinion that it could belong to the event of Joshua 24.[9] It could be said in favour of this view that it is here that the key word appears which expresses Yahweh's exclusive claim in the most striking manner: the reference to Yahweh as 'a jealous God'. In any case it is clear that this exclusiveness belongs essentially and unconditionally to belief in Yahweh as Israel understands it. The God who leads them out of Egypt suffers no other to be honoured as he is honoured.

Israel's belief is founded exclusively on this One. Her relationship to the world will be determined by the nature of her encounter with this One.

This means that Israel at her very beginnings, even at the beginnings of that group which transmitted its belief to the broader circle of the twelve tribes, was really involved in the events of her worldly history. The extraordinary event of the rescue at the Red Sea, when the Exodus group escaped from its Egyptian persecutors, was the occasion of the first song of praise of Yahweh which the Old Testament reports from Israel. It was sung by Moses and then by his sister Miriam, Exodus 15. The fire of Israel's first revolt against God was kindled in the very act of her delivery from Egypt; she drew back at the privations and harshness of the wandering: 'If only we had died at the Lord's hand in Egypt, where we sat round the flesh pots and had plenty of bread to eat!' This was the lament of the exhausted Israelites in the exacting life of the desert before Yahweh gave them the manna from heaven (Exod. 16.3; 17.3; Num. 11.5). And this same lament reached its climax of black despair in the conclusion in Numbers 14.3ff.: 'To go back to Egypt would be better than this. And they began to talk of choosing someone to lead them back.'

It is this point of contact with the concrete events of history that distinguishes Israel's faith; it is a faith far removed from any relationship to God which derives from philosophical reflection. Old Testament faith is not conditioned by or directed to the beyond, to something in the background which stands over against the concrete course of history. It remains bound to the experience of its own history both in song of praise and in revolt and knows that it is there that it meets its God.

The unequivocal nature of this relationship distinguishes the faith of Israel from that of its surrounding world, where the divinities, besides their relationship to the history of mankind, bear for the most part a relationship to the various phenomena of nature. Albrektson, to be sure, has recently directed our attention to the relationships which the divinities of Babylon and Assyria have to history and to the fact that they are experienced by their effects in the framework of history.[10] And this is quite impressive. However, the persistent and unequivocal relationship of Yahweh to the history of Israel, which is present from her earliest confession, and which impresses on this history in all its phases the action of the Lord who led them out of Egypt, and which never succumbed to the temptation to identify Yahweh with any of the powers of nature, is completely absent in the surrounding world. It is worth while to set this faith in somewhat sharper focus. Ernst Bloch has succeeded in giving the God of the Exodus greater influence and resonance even in the area of Christian theology. Bloch understands the Exodus as the principle by which one breaks free from and transcends the present situation with a view to new horizons.[11] But that is not what characterizes the Old Testament confession of the Exodus. The acknowledgement of Yahweh, who has led Israel out of Egypt, is not merely the acknowledgement of a power which is always giving a direction, always urging to leave behind the current situation and driving towards an ultimate goal which is the fulfilment of man's ideals. The Old Testament understands the Exodus event as an act of salvation, in which the central theme is not man's liberation of himself, but the mighty act of Yahweh who liberates from slavery and who in this act of liberation addresses his merciful acceptance to the one whom he calls. The Exodus which Yahweh effects is his act of mercy and not primarily a human accomplishment which results in liberation.

Israel, then, because she is bound to her history and to the secular involved in it, is not bound to any venerable principle of liberation; she is involved in a promise of the divine presence which will lead her in the events of the world in which she lives. It is a call to trust in this instruction which has come about in the course of history, an instruction which will persevere in the future, however different the way which is taken.

This is to be illustrated further by events narrated subsequently in the Old Testament. There is the story of Yahweh's constant concern and attention which the people experienced on their way through the sharp privations of the desert. When threatened with hunger and thirst, they were provided with food and drink. The caring hand of God was ever visible in these events; he protected them from the attacks of the hordes of the Amalekites (Exod. 17), and he sent down the manna for their daily food (Exod. 16).

The prayer from Deuteronomy 26.5–10a, which Gerhard von Rad has entitled 'Short Historical Credo',[12] plays an important role in recent pentateuchal research. Discussion of this prayer has made it quite clear that in its present form it is stamped with the Deuteronomic language and is a rubrical-liturgical piece of the seventh century B.C.[13] On the other hand it must be remembered that the prayer also contains traditional material which is older and which is not part of the Deuteronomic vocabulary. This seventh-century prayer is put on the lips of an Israelite farmer who enters the holy place at harvest time with a basket of produce freshly gathered from the fields; he hands it over to the priest while recalling in the presence of Yahweh:

> My father was a wandering Aramaean who went down to Egypt with a small company and lived there until they became a great, powerful, and numerous nation. But the Egyptians ill-treated us, humiliated us and imposed cruel slavery upon us. Then we cried to the Lord the God of our fathers for help, and he listened to us and saw our humiliation, our hardship and distress; and so the Lord brought us out of Egypt with a strong hand and outstretched arm, with terrifying deeds, and with signs and portents. He brought us to this place and gave us this land, a land flowing with milk and honey. And now I have brought the firstfruits of the soil which thou, O Lord, has given me.

The prayer which the farmer recites expresses a thoroughgoing concern with the gifts of the earth. The manner of his concern shows those same characteristics which, as we have just seen, belong to the foundations of the faith of Israel. As the farmer carried the produce of the soil in his basket, his thoughts would turn to the mysterious power of growth in the soil; he would be reminded of the showers of rain that had been sent by the heavenly powers to water the soil at the proper time. The devotee of the religion of Canaan, of Mesopotamia, or of Egypt would have seen the power of the nature divinities at work here and praised them. What a striking contrast is the prayer of the Israelite farmer. He does not waste a word on this. With the produce of the field before him, he thinks exclusively of his history: Yahweh, in an act of pure grace, has led him out of the oppression of Egypt into the abundance of this land, and has made it possible for him to bring to the sanctuary the fruit of the land 'which you, Yahweh, have given me'.

There are, of course, other prayers in the Old Testament which speak directly of the blessings of heaven and which see Yahweh alone at work in them.[14] This prayer, however, contains no fixed archaic formula from earlier times; it has been adapted to the language of the late monarchical period, and it brings out quite distinctly the main lines of the relationship between the Old Testament and the world. This prayer of the farmer does not address one who governs everything in a timeless cycle of eternal return or one who is quite removed from the course of time; it looks to the Lord who has accompanied and led this people since it began to become Israel, and who has blessed it yet again.

The theme of being with and leading the people dominates the whole of the Israel event with which the Old Testament, the book of the divine instruction of Israel, is concerned.[15] The period of the Judges, whose traditions have been reworked in its own peculiar way by the Deuteronomic school, is interpreted according to the pattern of the act of liberation at the beginning of the people's history. The story is always the same: Yahweh hears Israel's cry as she suffers, through her own fault, under the hand of her oppressors; he sends a saviour who liberates her. The history of Saul and David, the first kings of Israel, who freed the people from the oppression of the Philistines, can be interpreted in the same way.[16] But when the prophet Nathan, 2 Samuel 7, promises the house of David that it will last for ever, then a new element is added to the history of the kings of Israel. It is not an element, however, that calls the faith of Israel to look outside and beyond its world and history to something far off; rather it calls it to focus its attention on the event taking place in the king's house in the course of Yahweh's history.

The great prophets, whose words have come down to us in writing, stressed the very same with a force hitherto unheard. It is clear to the historian that in the period from the eighth century to the sixth century when the great prophets spoke, Palestine entered yet again into a long period of suffering as she was ground between the great powers. As the land-bridge between Asia and Africa she was the land which both the east and the south wanted to possess. In the rivalry between the great powers when first Assyria, then the new Babylonian kingdom and finally its Persian successor dominated the field, the small states on this land-bridge, which included both parts of greater Israel, were pulverized. It was a stormy period in which withdrawal from the world into a hidden inner faith could well have suggested itself. The great prophets were commissioned to prevent Israel from fleeing into such a retreat, which might end in some hidden interiorism or in the indifference of nihilism, and to make her encounter her God in the midst of the storms of that world. Isaiah sees Assyria as the instrument of God's angry judgement.[17] Jeremiah dares to describe the king of the new Babylonian empire, Nebuchadnezzar, as 'the servant of Yahweh'.[18] And Deutero-Isaiah, in proclaiming the good news of the imminent liberation, addresses the pagan king of the Persians, Cyrus, with the title of the anointed one, the Messiah of Yahweh.[19] Throughout the whole of this turbulent history the faith of Israel meets Yahweh in the full course of the events of the world. It is demanded of Israel that she stand firm with her God, bow to his judgement and wait his salvation. It is then more than mere chance that Deutero-Isaiah in his message of the coming liberation under Cyrus quite unexpectedly recalls the ancient image of God leading his people out of slavery. It is a quite exaggerated picture of a new Exodus in which the desert is changed to a festal processional way along which the people can return from Babylon to Zion, so as to lift up their voices once more in a new hymn of praise to Yahweh the king.[20]

It is a complete misunderstanding if one tries to see in this a mere nationalistic and secular vital force. It is Yahweh who is in action in this worldly event. It is not that history would become, as it were, an instrument with its own law for measuring God, as German Christian theology has continually tried to do, thinking that it can recognize God in history, and claiming him for its own in time of success. It is significant that Amos proclaimed his revolutionary message of judgement in the midst of an externally prosperous period of history, and that the loudest cry of triumph over the coming liberation echoed forth where Israel was no more and when she seemed to be destined to definitive destruction after decades of historical death. For the prophet history is the field where God acts freely, and one cannot simply read off his action from success and disaster. Yahweh's majesty has never been more enthusiastically glorified as when Israel, sunk in the depths of helplessness, waited in hope for her God.

God instructs the Old Testament believer by throwing him back on the events of the world; but God is not the world's servant nor is he bound by it; he remains always its sovereign disposer. The whole thrust of the Old Testament proclamation guards against any flight into a beyond which is turned away from the world; faith is established in the midst of the events of the world. One can see this too where the individual finds himself faced with the problem of his own personal world. The book of Job might be mentioned as an example. The first two chapters of the book describe graphically how one messenger after another announces the disasters which have come upon Job's property and family; Job finally falls helpless to the ground before God, yet he can still praise him through his suffering: 'The Lord gives and the Lord takes away; blessed be the name of the Lord.' The reader might pause a moment and ask if we have not here an example of the Stoic ideal of impassivity, *ataraxia*: the sufferer, who does not allow himself to be shaken in his suffering. But Job's speeches in the following chapters, with their indescribable struggle with the inexplicable, where he does not turn away from God but acknowledges him in the depths of the mystery that he is, tell a quite different story. Here too his faith cannot take refuge in flight from the trial which has come upon him. Here too he must stand firm with God in the events of his life and seek God out from the midst of this, his world of suffering.

The Old Testament does not proceed from the general to the particular, with the result that faith is ever able to save itself by recourse to the general. Faith encounters Yahweh in concrete events of history and binds man ever to these same events. Once this is acknowledged, then the next question can be put: how does the Old Testament speak of the very beginnings of the world, and how does faith view the world in this context?

2

THE WORLD AS GOD'S CREATION

Our question about 'the Old Testament and the world' has apparently caused us to make a detour. Our further question about the origins and 'world-orientation' of the instruction which Israel, the channel through which the Old Testament came to us, received from Yahweh her God, has taken us away from the place which we thought most suited to tell us something about the relationship between the Old Testament and the world, namely the accounts of the beginning of the world in Genesis. Israel knows the instruction of her God from her concrete encounter in the departure from Egypt, and she realizes that from that moment on she is thrown completely into the world history where she experiences the decisions of Yahweh.

Aware of this we must now turn our attention to those accounts of the beginning where the world in its whole extent is the object of biblical discussion. All the more so, because the conclusions we have reached about the use of the divine names do not do away with the impression that these accounts of the beginning are speaking of none other than the very God who, according to the Elohistic and priestly writings, begins to deal with Israel under his proper name of Yahweh only in the time of Moses.

A brief preliminary reflection from the viewpoint of the history of religions may be in place here and may help to clarify the matter. The group which experienced God's saving action in the departure from Egypt came into the land of Canaan; there, in the light of this experience, it articulated its faith in Yahweh and passed it on to the other groups with which it subsequently formed the twelve tribes of Israel. When this group entered Canaan, it entered a realm of spiritual experience which had already had much to say about the beginnings of the world and the world-

orientation of belief in God. The Ugaritic texts, though they
belong to the north of Syria where other influences were at work,
have illustrated graphically how ancient Canaan had quite a lot to
say about happenings between God and the world.[1] Even though
Ugarit itself has up to the present remained remarkably silent on
this matter, nevertheless, it has much to say about divinities
which had created the world. This is quite clear too from the Old
Testament itself in the account of Genesis 14. Abraham on his
return from rescuing Lot from the hands of the four kings of the
East meets King Melkizedek from Salem. There is no doubt that
the name Jerusalem lies hidden here. Melkizedek, who is
described as priest of *El Elyon*, presents Abraham with bread and
wine and blesses the ancestor of Israel with the words: 'Blessed be
Abram by God most high, creator of heaven and earth. And
blessed be God most high, who has delivered your enemies into
your power.' Abraham in response gives him a tenth of all he
possesses. This episode demonstrates beyond doubt that before
ever Israel took possession of Jerusalem under David, there was
honoured in the city a god with the name of *El Elyon*, of whom it
was said that he was the creator of heaven and earth.[2] Israel on
settling in the land encountered such claims on behalf of the local
deities and could not avoid facing the question whether she would
acknowledge these claims or reject them. Is there to be a quite
amicable and reasonable arrangement whereby a divinity like *El
Elyon*, creator of heaven and earth, is given a place beside
Yahweh, so that while Yahweh remains the liberator of the Exodus,
the creation of the world is ascribed to *El Elyon*? One meets
everywhere in the world which surrounds Israel such specializa-
tion on the part of the divinities together with belief in one God, a
God who in particular has to do with the creation of the world.
One expects, however, something quite different from Israel's
quite exclusive faith, which acknowledges that Yahweh endures
no other to take a stand by him. In this new perspective, where a
new question has arisen, and Israel is faced with the problem of
the creator of the world, she can only answer that there can ob-
viously be no other Lord than Yahweh. It is interesting therefore
to see how the story of Genesis 14 continues; Abraham takes an
oath in the name of Yahweh his God; and he quite calmly and
naturally ascribes to Yahweh not merely the attributes but also
the very name of the God of Melkizedek: 'I lift my hand and swear

by the Lord, God most high, creator of heaven and earth . . .' ('God most high' is the translation of *El Elyon*). This is the beginning of Abraham's oath in verse 22. Yahweh's activity experiences thereby a broader interpretation in the context of the creator of the world. And so Yahweh has become the divine Lord declared responsible for the creation of the world, long before he had to come to terms with the claim of Jerusalem's revered *El Elyon* in the time of David. This is the situation in Genesis 1. Moreover, Genesis 1 shows that Israel never developed a unified presentation of the creation of the world; no such presentation prevailed as was the case with the account of Israel's liberation from Egypt where all sources maintained, in their broad lines, the same pattern, which has something of a credal-type unity about it. One can recognize in the beginning of Genesis two very different accounts of the beginning of the world, different both in general form and in detail. *El Elyon* was the opposing deity of Jerusalem; it is no longer possible to determine which were the opposing deities of the surrounding world against whom these two creation accounts were formed. However, the different forms of the creation accounts at the beginning of Genesis enable us to recognize quite clearly—and this is the reverse of Genesis 14 where all is darkness—the geographical background in which the details of both creation presentations have grown up.

The older of the two narratives which begins in Genesis 2.5 comes from the Yahwist. As we have seen, it used the name of Yahweh quite naturally for the creation event.[3] In a detailed, picturesque, and highly elaborate series of articulated sentences, the account runs:

> When the Lord God made earth and heaven, there was neither shrub nor plant growing wild upon the earth, because the Lord God had sent no rain on the earth; nor was there any man to till the ground . . . Then the Lord God formed a man from the dust of the ground and breathed into his nostrils the breath of life. Thus the man became a living creature.

The speaker here is one in whose view desert and dryness were the necessary data when he attempts to present the beginning when there was no life. He thinks that the world took its shape from a beginning such as this. The more perceptive will see here two quite different lines of presentation: the one in which God causes it to rain over this dryness, the other, betraying a more marked mythical background, according to which a stream of water bursts forth from the deep; but this need not be pursued any further here. There can scarcely be any doubt that the speaker here is a man from the dry interior, from the country area of Syria–Palestine.[4]

The account of Genesis 1.1–2.4a is on the contrary quite different. It is the well-known account of God's work of six days which concludes with the rest on the sabbath. This latter is but one indication that here a priestly writer is speaking. It is the high point of the priestly writing in which the name of Yahweh is first revealed to Moses and which, in the period before Abraham, speaks of Elohim, 'God'. The beginning should be translated by a rather formal period, in a way similar to the stylized beginning of the Yahwistic account, and so differently from the versions usually given: 'In the beginning of creation, when God made heaven and earth, the earth was without form and void, with darkness over the face of the abyss and a mighty wind that swept over the surface of the waters. God said, "Let there be light", and there was light . . .' This is a voice from a world which can present the beginnings of all things, when there was neither form nor life, only as the dark, restless, miry waters of chaos. It is the world picture of the river plains where each year after the rainy reason the land lies under water and life can only be reawakened when the waters are driven back. And this will be the great work of the second and third days of creation after the darkness has been dispelled in the work of the first day. It is a situation familiar to the Nile valley and Mesopotamia, with the annual flooding of the rivers. The Phoenician cosmogony of Sanchuniaton which has come to us through Berossus and Eusebius, and which shows the very same elements, demonstrates that the basic presentations of the beginnings of the world have migrated from the river plains to Phoenician Canaan.[5] If Israel did not first encounter these presentations of the beginning of the world when she went into exile in Babylon, then she would have received them through Phoenician and Canaanite sources.

It is necessary to make yet another explanation before proceeding any further. Hitherto, much has been said of the world picture, of the cosmology of the Phoenicians and of the accounts of the creation of the world at the beginning of the Old Testament.

One who has paid close attention to the citations from the beginning of both of the creation narratives will be struck by the fact that the expression 'world' is lacking. The Yahwist has written: 'When the Lord God made earth and heaven . . .'; the priestly writer has said: 'In the beginning of creation when God made heaven and earth . . .'. Where we simply say 'world', these two accounts have spoken of heaven and earth or of earth and heaven, in each case in a different order. And this is the case throughout the whole of the Old Testament. It is not yet familiar with the notion 'world'.[6] This notion clearly implies order which seeks to embrace the whole, a whole which the Old Testament describes piecemeal by naming the two most important sections of the world. It corresponds to the Greek notion of cosmos. The idea of order is central to *cosmos*, and with it is also linked the notion of the beautiful (*cosmos* is the word which describes a woman's make-up and dress). It is the Ionic nature-philosophy that passes on this notion of order to the whole world complex, which is held together by its own order. Cosmos is the world system held together by its own internal order. It is in this way that Plato understands the All (*to holon, to pan*), every individual thing and individual being, heaven and earth, gods and men as bound together in unity by a universal order, something like an animated body.

> For this our Cosmos has received the living creatures both mortal and immortal and been thereby fulfilled; it being itself a visible Living Creature embracing the visible creatures, a perceptible God made in the image of the Intelligible, most great and good and fair and perfect in its generation—even this one Heaven sole of its kind.[7]

Leaving aside the idea of the world soul, Aristotle too speaks of the cosmos as the all-embracing, besides which there is no other conscious world whole. When Plato in *Timaeus* 28ff. appoints a *demiurge* as 'maker and father' to rule his cosmos, which is itself divine, then there is a lack of balance, and this is excluded by Aristotle when he deals with the possibility of the cosmos having no beginning and no end.[8]

This thought pattern is completely unknown to the Old Testament. The world in the Old Testament is never a self-contained whole; rather the whole comprises the different parts which have been created. The world can perhaps be described as 'the whole, all' in one of the creation formulas in Isaiah 44.24: 'I am the Lord who made all things, by myself I stretched out the skies, alone I hammered out the floor of the earth."[9] This 'all' is quite opposed to the Greek notion of cosmos and order and quite foreign to any sort of divine self-sufficiency before Yahweh. Later Judaism, under the influence of Greek civilization, used the word *'olam* to describe the world. More important on the other hand was the assumption of the notion of cosmos into the post-canonical hellenistic Jewish writings. The second book of Maccabees, 7.23, can describe God as 'creator of the cosmos'. It must be stated quite clearly here, and this is important for everything that follows, that when we speak in a general way of 'the world', then this is to be clearly distinguished from the Greek notion of cosmos, and is always to be understood in the Old Testament sense of 'heaven and earth' as in Genesis 1.1.

With this explanation made with regard to the Greek understanding of the cosmos, the further question can arise, how the two creation narratives at the beginning of the Old Testament understand 'heaven and earth', and what directions these creation stories give for the relationship between the world and man. It will be worth while then to cast a glance at Israel's immediate neighbours in the Ancient Near East.

The best known literary composition is Enuma Elish, commonly known as the Babylonian creation epic. It begins with a detailed succession of those very negatives which occur in the subordinate clauses of the biblical texts. The world picture is that of Genesis 1:

> When on high the heaven had not been named,
> Firm ground below had not been called by name,
> Naught but primordial Apsu, their begetter,
> (And) Mummu-Tiamat, she who bore them all,
> Their waters co-mingling as a single body;
> No reed hut had been matted, no marsh land had appeared,
> When no gods whatever had been brought into being,
> Uncalled by name, their destinies undetermined—
> Then it was that the gods were formed within them.[10]

After a series of generations of the gods with all sorts of intervening episodes, it finally comes to a confrontation between the ancient divinities of chaos and the young god Marduk, the god of the city of Babylon and the national god of the Babylonian empire.

Marduk slays Tiamat in the battle and out of the two halves of her severed body builds heaven and earth. Man is created out of the blood of Tiamat's paramour, Kingu. This last motif appears in a different form in another fragment where the mother goddess Ninhursag mixes the blood of one of the murdered gods with clay and forms man with it.[11]

One can recognize quite clearly in these selections from a wide variety of examples in Israel's surrounding world three markedly different approaches to the origin of the world and what it contains.[12] First, there is the idea of origin through generation. Enuma Elish uses this image to describe the origin of the succession of divinities out of Tiamat, the maternal monster of primeval chaos. This same image occurs in other places as well, for example, in Sumerian and Egyptian, as well as in Phoenician mythology, when they present the origin of other elements of the world.[13] A further leading motif in Enuma Elish is that of the struggle of the creator god with the representatives of chaos. Creation is wrested from chaos in a victorious struggle. The origins are presented thirdly through the image of the craftsman; the world, and all that is in it, is simply made. Heaven and earth are built out of the corpse of Tiamat. Man is formed from clay and the blood of a god. We are familiar with the Egyptian figure of Chnum, the ram-headed god from Elephantine, who forms the Pharaoh and his Ka on the potter's wheel.[14] There is yet a fourth way of presenting creation that has claimed attention in recent years, namely, creation by the word, by no means unknown among Israel's neighbours. There is the case of Hike, the god of magic in Egypt; when he is addressed as the creator one thinks of the power of his magical word.[15] But much more impressive is the document that records what is called the theology of Memphis: what is clearly a very ancient text attributes the origin not only of the gods, but of everything else in the world, to what Ptah conceives in his heart and orders with his tongue.[16] The decision of the heart and the commanding speech are the real forces of creation.

Israel's surrounding world had already shaped a great deal of linguistic material and imagery to express the relationship of God or the gods to the 'heaven and earth', the ALL, or what might be called the 'world'. Israel had no need to create the language in which she had to speak.[17] We must now examine more closely how Israel used the linguistic devices which had been passed on to her.

The narrative of the Yahwist claims first attention. Three aspects of his narrative style deserve special attention. First, and in a quite striking manner, the narrator prefaces his presentation of the 'not yet formed', which opens the Babylonian epic, with a short introductory sentence which sets everything in proper perspective: 'When the Lord God made earth and heaven . . .' The following verses deal with the action by which the ALL came from the hand of Yahweh alone. This is very different from the presentation of the beginning among Israel's neighbours in that there is no preliminary theogony, nor is it necessary to describe the subordination of the world of the subsidiary gods to the creator. Neither does it enter the mind of the narrator to engage in any polemics to the effect that this creator is to be claimed as the self-generator, as was done on behalf of the Egyptian Chepren.[18] It is simply and solemnly taken for granted that the Lord God is there and that whatever else is there, be it world, earth and heaven, comes from him.

Secondly, one is struck by the calm indifference with which the narrator passes over the gap which the perceptive analyst would easily notice: the gap, that is, between the assertion that the Lord God made heaven and earth, and the point of departure, which is an already existing unwatered and barren desert waste. The earth, which the antecedent sentence assures us is made by the Lord God, is clearly not really earth, as long as Yahweh has not set to work on it. His picture of the world causes him no difficulty.

Thirdly, there is the artless unconcern with which the Yahwist describes Yahweh's action as he creates and shapes that part of the world which is of such importance for him. Yahweh shapes the man out of the moist earth, just as the potter Chnum had shaped man's body on his wheel. Like an orchardist he plants the garden of delight in which he puts the man into whom he had breathed his own life-giving breath. And again like the potter he forms from clay all the beasts of the field and the birds of the heaven, and he brings them to the man to try out and to see if he can find a helper among them which is suited to him. And then we have his compassionate reflection: 'It is not good for the man to be alone, I will provide a partner for him.' And just as a master builder builds a house out of the appropriate material, so Yahweh builds the woman out of the rib which he has taken from the sleeping man, acting like a mason who closes over a breach in a wall, closing over with flesh the wound which has been made in the body of the man. The woman is now the person who is a suitable partner for the man and she is greeted by him with the joyful cry: 'Now this at last—bone from my bones, flesh from my flesh—this shall be called woman, for from man was this taken.' The goal, to make all good for man, has now been reached.

The great event of the creation of heaven and earth by the Lord God emerges only episodically in the Yahwist's narrative of God's creative work. But one can recognize all the more clearly in the passage which the author makes the highlight of his narrative what he intends to say about the relationship between the world and man. According to the Yahwist, everything that Yahweh creates on this day converges on the man: the garden is created for the man; Yahweh experiments with the beasts for the man's good. Yahweh's intention finally reaches its goal with the woman. The man, in accordance with the conclusive will of Yahweh, is completely geared to what has been created for him in the world, so that he may be a complete man of the world in the enjoyment of what he has received.

The priestly account of the creation of the world precedes the Yahwistic account. Its stiff stylization, which borders on the monotonous, its ponderousness, and its lack of imagery are quite different from the colourful, unaffected, and picturesque narrative of the Yahwist. However, they are not without points of contact. Here too an assuring introductory headline is set above the whole: 'In the beginning of creation, when God made heaven and earth.' The Yahwist had used the ordinary simple verb for human activity, 'make'; in the priestly writing there occurs the more specific verb, 'create', *bara'*. A review of the not too frequent occurrences of this verb in the Old Testament shows that it is never used with any other subject than Yahweh. And never does this verb presume any material out of which Yahweh creates. Whatever the original, and perhaps more graphic, meaning of the word may have been,[19] it is reserved in the Old Testament for the creative act of God to which there is no corresponding human act and which stands above any human activity. The priestly writing is basically different from the unsophisticated language of the Yahwist. One should remember, however, that the gap between Yahweh's incomparable act of creation which needs no pre-existing matter, and the primeval waters of darkness which, as the narrative proceeds, are clearly there, is not closed.

All subsequent accounts of Yahweh's activity are subordinated to his word, even when the word remains in the background and is linked with an expression describing his 'dividing' or 'making'.[20] This word differs from the word in the ancient theology of Memphis in that it continues effective through the priestly narrative directing history towards its goal; it looks not only to the covenant with Noah and to the later one with Abraham the ancestor of Israel, but reaches into the very heart of the history of the people of Israel in the time of Moses. Speculation about the creative activity of Ptah attained such a sublime level that both the will and command of the god reveal themselves in it; whereas the priestly reflection lives from the word of God in creation, and through and beyond this from the concrete experience that the call and command of Yahweh have determined and continue to determine the whole of Israel's life on her way through history.

Further, the priestly creation account reveals a decisive will of the highest integrity. One part of the world after another, heaven, earth, sea, comes into existence at the divine call. Everything which the Greeks see bound together in the cosmos as a divinely animated unity (so Plato) comes into existence here at God's call; and God stands over against this all and everything. Those powers of nature which Israel's neighbours believed to be surrounded by divine mystery and for that reason deserving of awesome respect, come into existence in Genesis 1 in obedience to God's command. The sun, the moon, and the heavenly bodies are what they are only because the creator has called them into existence. One cannot miss the quiet polemic against the awe which surrounds these astral bodies. Their very names, Sun (*Shemesh*) and Moon (*Yareah*), by which Israel's neighbours designate certain gods, are avoided; instead they are almost contemptuously described as the greater light and the lesser light. These powers become instruments. Their function is limited strictly to service, 'to govern day and night, and to separate light from darkness' (v. 18).

But the great question that our theme raises is the question of man. What does the priestly account have to say about man and his relationship to the world which has been created; about that special freedom from the powers of the cosmos which is his, and which must clearly be conceded to him in treating of the great astral powers?

Two things must be recognized here, each in its own peculiar way. On the one hand man is completely taken up into the created world, which has its existence from its creator. At the same time, however, man is elevated in a quite special way and is different from all other creatures. All other works of creation are introduced and called into being one after the other by God's commanding word; the creation of man begins with the divine reflection: 'Let us make man in our image and likeness.' And the effect of man's special likeness to God is unfolded immediately: he is 'to rule the fish in the sea, the birds of heaven, the cattle, all wild animals on earth, and all reptiles that crawl upon the earth'.

At the same time, however, man is once more set in relationship to these creatures. The blessing of fertility is given both to man and to each of these creatures: 'Be fruitful and increase, fill the earth.' Man is given the commission to rule: 'Subdue it.' Man then is bound to the world in two different ways: he is incorporated into it, and he is to rule over it. Each of these relationships must be discussed in its proper place. One of the themes of Genesis 1 is that of the praise of the world which God has created. The work of each day concludes with the remark: 'And God saw that it was good.'[21] And at the conclusion of the work of creation there is the fuller summing up: 'And God saw all that he had made, and it was very good.'[22]

Ernst Bloch has sharply rejected this praise of creation. His judgement on Genesis 1 is: 'The god of the Babylonian empire, Marduk, came as the author of order to Ptah the author of the world. The noble regent of the cosmos to the noble founder of the cosmos, completing without a mistake all that concerns the prelude to and the beginning of the world.'[23] He sees here the proclamation of a god who is the rival of the god of the Exodus, the justification of the one who of his nature exists and perseveres in this existence. But is that what the priestly narrative is saying about the creation of the world?

Bloch's polemic completely isolates what Genesis 1 says from what the priestly writer has to say later in his narrative. Genesis 1.1–2.4a, with its presentation of the first week of the created world (a world which is not the Greek cosmos with its harmonious order), forms the entrance to a path leading to the shocking statement of 6.12 which clearly refers back to 1.31: 'In his sight the world had become corrupted, for all men had lived corrupt lives on earth.' The priestly writer is aware of the goodness of the beginning which is there no more. When one speaks of the great blessings of the command 'be fruitful and increase', as well as of the dominion conferred on man, one must also speak of this other side. But the priestly writer knows well that even when the world has become ambiguous, then neither is the blessing nor the call into the world muted.

What the priestly writer has set down in the brief remark of 6.11 is described in great detail in the Yahwistic narrative. He moves without any indignation from the account of man's sin in the garden of paradise. And the stories which the Yahwist joins together right up to chapter 11 illustrate with examples the extraordinary variety of ways in which man can revolt against God and the sad consequences of such revolts.[24]

It is from this world with all its riches that Yahweh has meant man to enjoy—from the tree in the middle of the garden, which God has reserved to himself to be a continual reminder to man of the giver of all gifts, that temptation stirs. It seems to be no more than a matter of a small and attractive piece of fruit. It seems so incidental, so unimportant. But it is the tempter who is the interpreter of the event, and who brings to light the unfathomable depths of the conflict that goes on in the man, who reveals the deeper meaning of what it is all about: 'God knows that as soon as you eat it, your eyes will be opened and you will be like gods knowing both good and evil.' To be like God, that is the real temptation that confronts the man here. To have no further need of God as Lord, to be of the world without God—this is how the fruit of the tree in the middle of the garden appears to man.

The story of the Tower of Babel is saying the same in different words and imagery.[25] Men have gathered together and live side by side. They will no longer live in the uncertainty of vagrants. They will build a city, a mighty creation of their own which will hold them together; and a tower by which they will be able to climb up to heaven. Man is equivocal in his relationship to the world.

These stories point not only to the misuse of the world which God has created for man; they are at the same time a reminder of that unique freedom which the creator has conferred upon man when setting him in the world, as well as of his elevation above other creatures. Should one, with H. E. Tödt, speak of man as 'God's ever open-ended experiment'?[26] The Old Testament is concerned with this creature, man, at the same time ennobled and endangered by his own freedom, yet destined to full involvement in the world.

3

BE FRUITFUL
AND INCREASE, AND FILL
THE EARTH

The reflections on the accounts of creation which were gathered together in the previous chapter in the context of the relationship of the Old Testament to the world, have led to the somewhat surprising conclusion that Old Testament thought has no equivalent of the notion of cosmos. 'The world' is never understood in the Old Testament as a self-contained organism which follows its own internal laws of order. It has not been necessary therefore to encompass this whole with one single word.

However, the priestly account of the beginning of the creation of heaven and earth is by no means lacking in elements of order. Like the work of an architect, the whole is built from the foundations up. This world structure, so carefully constructed from its cosmic ground plan up, is ever more richly furnished in what follows. It proceeds through the plants and the beasts to man. This notion of development, according to which the world is gradually built up from its beginnings to a richly articulated whole, is to be strictly respected. The carefully constructed edifice, the abundant fullness, remains subordinate to God's command and call.

The self-sufficient life of beast and man requires special attention in this context. Over and above the divine call to existence there comes the twofold word of blessing. 'Be fruitful and increase' is pronounced over man and beast alike. It then ramifies. God pronounces further over the fish and the birds: 'Be fruitful and increase, fill the waters of the seas; and let the birds increase on the land.' And he says to man: 'Fill the earth and subdue it, rule over the fish in the sea, the birds of heaven, and every living thing that moves upon the earth.' The absence of a similar command to the beasts of the land, which were created immediately before man on the sixth day, would be due to stylistic reasons. This same pronouncement is made over the beasts of the land when the blessing is renewed after the flood (Gen. 9.1, 7).

There is behind this priestly formulation the sense of wonder at the power of propagation and fertility not merely of the animals, but also of man. The power to generate the species and so to multiply visibly man and beast was not just taken for granted as something obvious; it was experienced as something to marvel at. This experience would confirm the Greek mind in its reflection on the cosmos. But what a mysterious order is at work in these phenomena. Old Testament faith speaks of God's blessing in this context.[1]

The pronouncement and the act of blessing are no longer current in our modern day-to-day life. Primitive religious belief shows a firm conviction that when people are near to death, potentates, kings, priests, and ordinary mortals too, certain words together with certain actions can pass on to the receiver powers which give him length of life and which guarantee him abundance and fulfilment; for example, the laying on of the right hand. In Israel one can speak neither of blessing, nor of its opposite, curse, without reference to the Lord, to whom all power belongs.[2] It is just as impossible to bless as to curse contrary to his will. This is demonstrated from certain Old Testament stories which seem to have retained fully the idea of the power of the word of the one who blesses or curses. For example, in Genesis 27, Isaac is old and blind; without wishing to do so, he blessed his son Jacob instead of Esau whom he really wanted to bless. His blessing could not be withdrawn. In the midst of all the human confusion and contriving that surrounds this story, what happened was what Yahweh, in accordance with his mysterious decision, wanted to happen; it was quite contrary to the decisions of man. In Numbers 22–4, the king of Moab knew that the foreign seer Balaam was possessed of certain power to pronounce a curse; he summoned him and commissioned him to curse Israel; but Balaam, contrary to the intention of the king and his own intention, had to bless Israel. And so he fulfilled the will of one who disposes of all power and who had called Israel as his own chosen people.

Such human mediators of blessing do not appear in the creation stories. It is the creator himself who pronounces the blessing, and in the act of pronouncing it he fills parts of the world which he has created with the power to dispose of it in mysterious ways. The blessing then is not something beyond the confines of the world. It is injected into the midst of the world, into the life of man and beast in this world. The man of faith of the Old Testament hears God's word of blessing as the priestly writer speaks of the phenomenon of fertility and abundance; and he realizes that with it he is directed once more into the midst of the visible world.

Modern thinking about the cosmos takes basically the same line as Greek thought; it sees here the forces of nature and regards the world as a self-contained life cycle disposing of its own internal powers. There belongs to this life cycle not only the fertility and generative power of man and beast, but also the power which gives growth to the plants. It is appropriate therefore to examine the manner in which the priestly writer understands the secret of the growth of plant life, which is there in the created world and which man realizes he must not overlook. The manner in which he speaks of this growth will throw further light on his understanding of the world to which man belongs.

The origin of the plant world is described in the context of the work of the third day, in which the sea and the land are separated from each other. At the beginning stands the divine command: 'Let the earth produce fresh growth, let there be on the earth plants bearing seed, fruit trees bearing fruit[3] each with seed according to its kind.' The marvel of fertility and of increase by means of seed is fully recorded in this sentence, even though the way in which this is effected seems quite different from the case of man and beast. Here the earth acts as mediator; plants and trees take firm root in it and cannot free themselves from it to walk about like the animals and man. The earth is commanded to bring forth plants from itself. This manner of speaking reveals a traditional presentation which was known to Israel's neighbours; it is the idea of the divine earth. In Babylon it is Enlil who is the power that has to do with the earth. In Egypt the earth was produced by the god Geb. There is the Greek story of 'mother earth' which is embodied in Demeter, the patroness of fertility and plant growth. When she hides herself after the rape of Persephone by Pluto, the earth can no longer bear any fruit. It is only a short step from here to the idea of mother nature bearing fruit of herself. What is significant too is the way in which the biblical writer speaks of this part of the world as it brings forth in its mysterious way plants and fruit trees. It cannot do this by virtue of some god-like quality of its own; it is God's command that has given it the power and laid upon it the obligation to produce. Once again the idea of a self-contained cosmos is rejected, and all life and power and increase are derived from the powerful command of him who alone is powerful.

Here the two domains of the fertile world meet. It is not nature, it is not an animated cosmos that enables the earth to bring forth plants, and animals and men to be fruitful and to multiply; it is the divine creative word that has opened up these hidden powers.

The wonder which lies behind Genesis 1, an apparently quite factual account of the beginning of things, is developed in another place in a hymn of praise:

> For this is thy provision for it,
> watering its furrows, levelling its ridges,
> softening it with showers and blessing its growth.
> Thou dost crown the year with thy good gifts
> and the palm-trees drip with sweet juice;
> the pastures in the wild are rich with blessing
> and the hills wreathed in happiness,
> the meadows are clothed with sheep
> and the valleys mantled in corn,
> so that they shout, they break into song (Ps. 65.10–13).[4]

This is the world to which man too belongs as the communicator of the blessing: 'Be fruitful and increase.'

The Old Testament sees man as belonging fully to the world when it has him sharing fully in the blessing which is bestowed upon the animal kingdom. There must, of course, be a separate discussion about that privilege of man, by virtue of which he is made into the image of God and given special dominion.[5] Nowhere, however, does the Old Testament show any sign of a dualistic tendency to separate man from his solidarity with the animal kingdom, which like him was formed by Yahweh from the dust of the earth. And nowhere is there any sign of man taking refuge in some sort of superior intellectual existence, which would reject his link with the animals, neither in what they share corporeally, nor in what they share by virtue of the blessing which brings fertility. The Yahwist ventured to narrate that Yahweh actually experimented with the animals and tried to see if man could find among them a helper suited to him. The righteous man of

Proverbs 12.10 cares for his beast, and the law-giver directs: 'You shall not muzzle an ox while he is treading out the corn' (Deut. 25.4).

But man is summoned not only to stand in awe before the marvel of fertility which unites him with the animal kingdom. The divine blessing is formulated in an imperative: 'Be fruitful and increase.' Old Testament faith is ever conscious that this imperative represents fertility and the power to propagate not as something fated to occur, but as something to which man must give an approving 'yes'. The man of the Old Testament takes it for granted, and quite soberly, that he is called to marriage, to a life of sexual union between husband and wife. The idea that celibacy, abstention from marriage, could be something spiritually loftier, drawing man closer to God, is quite foreign to the Old Testament.

It is not necessary here to refer to the cultic-ritual prescriptions which speak of a woman's monthly period and a man's seminal emission as an area of uncleanness,[6] and which demand abstention from sexual union before feasts or before going to battle.[7] These are ancient taboos, coming from a more primitive era, which regard the realm of death and of sexual intercourse as areas where certain powers lurk, and which have led to the observance of certain precautionary practices of purification. These surround Israel's cultic life. It is of significance that they nowhere lead to any basic questioning of marriage and the begetting of children. It is taken for granted and without question that the high priest of the later priestly ranks will be married; the office demands hereditary succession.[8] Even where we encounter such groups as the Nazirites[9] and the Rechabites,[10] who observe temporary abstinence, celibacy plays no role at all. When one individual, Jeremiah, is commanded to remain celibate (Jer. 16.2), Yahweh says to him: 'You shall not marry a wife; you shall have neither son nor daughter in this place.' This is something quite different and refers to the catastrophe which was about to befall the land.

> For these are the words of the Lord concerning sons and daughters born in this place, the mothers who bear them and the fathers who beget them in this land: When men die, struck down by deadly ulcers, there shall be no wailing for them and no burial; they shall be like dung lying upon the ground. When men perish by sword or famine, their corpses shall become food for birds and for beasts (Jer. 16.3–4).

And when the prophet Hosea puts the adulterous wife whom he had married under severe restrictions and gives the order: 'Many a long day you shall live in my house and not play the wanton, and have no intercourse with a man, nor I with you',[11] then this is a temporary corrective measure arising out of a particular situation.

The man of the Old Testament knows that marriage is his normal state. This is true too for situations such as those envisaged by Jeremiah in the letter which he wrote to those who had been deported to Babylon in the year 597: 'Build houses and live in them; plant gardens and eat their produce. Marry wives and beget sons and daughters; take wives for your sons and give your daughters to husbands, so that they may bear sons and daughters and you may increase there and not dwindle away' (Jer. 29.5–6). Light, however indirect, is thrown on the obligation to see that there are children by the legal form of Levirite marriage, a practice quite strange to us. According to this, when a man dies childless, his brother is obliged to marry the wife of the deceased (multiple marriage is no problem in the Old Testament) and if possible to beget a son by her, who will bear the name of his deceased brother. The refusal to carry out this obligation towards one's deceased brother is stigmatized as shameful conduct by the law of Levirite marriage in Deuteronomy 25.8–10:

> If he still stands his ground and says, 'I will not take her', his brother's widow shall go up to him in the presence of the elders; she shall pull his sandal off his foot and spit in his face and declare: 'Thus we requite the man who will not build up his brother's family.'

The story of Onan too (Gen. 38.8ff.), who in these circumstances maliciously prevents Tamar from conceiving a child by him, and so is struck down by God, throws light on the attitude of Israel to marriage and posterity.

It is the normal thing for a husband to take pleasure in his family and to see in it God's blessing. The Psalms describe very vividly the blessing which Yahweh will give to the one who fears him:

> Your wife shall be like a fruitful vine
> in the heart of your house;
> your sons shall be like olive-shoots
> round about your table (Ps. 128.3).

And the preceding Psalm praises quite realistically the value of the gift of sons from Yahweh, even in life's conflicts:

> Sons are a gift from the Lord
> and children a reward from him.
> Like arrows in the hand of a fighting man
> are the sons of man's youth.
> Happy is the man
> who has his quiver full of them;
> such men shall not be put to shame
> when they confront their enemies in court (Ps. 127.3–5).

However, it would be undermining the value of marriage if it were to be regarded merely as a means of gaining the blessing of children. The Old Testament is well aware of the human richness in the meeting of man and woman. We can recall again the loud and joyful cry of man which the Yahwist records in his story of the beginnings when Yahweh brings the woman to him: 'Now this at last—bone from my bones, flesh from my flesh.' And man gives his own name to the woman when he continues: 'This shall be called woman, for from man was this taken' (woman, *'ishshah*; man, *'ish*).[12] And when the narrator continues: 'That is why a man leaves his father and mother and is united to his wife, and the two become one flesh', then he is referring not merely to the quite natural and physical union of man and woman, but also to their inner drive for companionship. It demands of man that, for the sake of his wife, he leave the whole structure which binds him to his family. This striking formulation, that it is the man and not the woman who leaves family, and which clearly runs quite contrary to patriarchal practice, is to stress in unmistakable terms the basic power of love.

The patriarchal history is saying the same thing when it describes Jacob's love for Rachel. 'So Jacob worked seven years for Rachel, and they seemed like a few days because he loved her' (Gen. 29.20). And when his father-in-law Laban shabbily deceives him and gives him Leah whom he does not love, then Jacob serves yet another seven years for Rachel, whom he loves. But it is the most 'worldly' book of the Old Testament, the Song of Songs, that highlights the love between man and woman. It has been taken into the canon only in its religious interpretation. The Song of Songs, which is one of the five scrolls, and which is read at the feast of the Pasch, is a collection of artistically arranged love songs. The art form is that of the 'travesty', that is, giving the characters strange and quickly changing roles. In the Song of Songs the characters play the role of king as well as the role of shepherd or gardener. The same art form had long been used in Egyptian love songs.[13] With a daring which is not found anywhere else in the Old Testament, the beauty of the loved ones and of love is described, with now the man now the woman speaking:

> No, a lily among thorns
> is my dearest among girls.
> Like an apricot-tree among the trees of the wood,
> so is my beloved among boys.
> To sit in its shadow was my delight,
> and its fruit was sweet to my taste (2.2–3).

> Wear me as a seal upon your heart,
> as a seal upon your arm;
> for love is strong as death,
> passion cruel as the grave;
> it blazes up like blazing fire,
> fiercer than any flame.
> Many waters cannot quench love,
> no flood can sweep it away;
> if a man were to offer for love
> the whole wealth of his house,
> it would be utterly scorned (8.6–7).[14]

Besides the allegorical interpretations there have been attempts right up to the present to interpret the Song of Songs in a mythical-cultic sense. It is said that it is the ritual text of a divine marriage.[15] But these interpretations have not been convincing. What is peculiar to the songs of this book is their decisive, unmythological secularity. The judgement of Gilles Gerleman is that 'there is not so much as a word or a suggestion that these experiences of love have been framed in a religious setting'.[16] Nevertheless there is expressed in the Song of Songs, and in what it says of love and sexuality, something which is quite in the spirit of the Old Testament. This whole aspect of life is 'the world', in the sense in which the world appears in the creation stories: something created, shaped by the creator, living and called into life by his word of blessing, never idealized in the name of religion nor misunderstood as part of the life of God.

This part of the created 'world', which makes no claim to any independence as something apart under its own separate and god-like system of law, and which is not to be understood in some completely self-enclosed theory of vitalism, is granted to man as a divine gift and blessing; he receives it as part of the joy which has been guaranteed to creation. This is the way in which the Preacher understands it, despite all his groaning over the fact that one cannot manipulate creation. When God guarantees man this joy at the time which he in his hidden wisdom has determined, then man should take pleasure in it:

> Go to it then, eat your food and enjoy it, and drink your wine with a cheerful heart; for already God has accepted what you have done. Always be dressed in white and never fail to anoint your head. Enjoy life with a woman you love all the days of your allotted span here under the sun, empty as they are; for that is your lot while you live and labour here under the sun (Eccles. 9.7–9).

The legal code of the book of Deuteronomy contains laws which regulate the preparations for war. They are expressed in a quite legal style. The officer addresses the army as it prepares for the campaign, in the following manner: 'Any man who has pledged himself to take a woman in marriage and has not taken her shall go back home; or he may die in battle and another man take her' (Deut. 20.7). And this is stated even more clearly in Deuteronomy 24.5: 'When a man is newly married, he shall not be liable for military service or any other public duty. He shall remain at home exempt from service for one year and enjoy the wife he has taken.'

Marriage and love are patently secular areas. They are worldly, not divine domains. They are, nevertheless, and of their very nature, domains of responsibility before God who has guaranteed this blessing. This is clear from the Old Testament. It is precisely because fertility and marriage are considered as natural gifts bestowed on the creature (nature not being understood in any ideological sense of self-sufficiency), that the Old Testament reacts very sharply against any unnatural perversion of these God-given gifts. According to Kurt Elliger, Leviticus 18 is basically an enumeration of the degrees of relationship within which sexual union is forbidden where large family groups live together; it is supplemented by strict regulations against sexual intercourse between people of the same sex and against bestiality

(Lev. 18.22ff.).[17] One might ask here whether the intention were not to reject certain practices which had won some sort of religious approval in the surrounding cultures. For that is the other frontier where one had to be on the alert—the religious idealizing of Eros which was in vogue in the Canaanite cults where women (and men?) gave themselves over to the sanctuary. Sayings such as 'that is not done in Israel'[18] or 'that is an abomination in Israel'[19] are ancient formulas by which Israel, Yahweh's people (2 Sam. 13.12; Gen. 34.7; Deut. 22.21; Judg. 20.6, 10; Jer. 29.23), set herself apart from her Canaanite neighbours. The story of the corruption of the people of Sodom in Genesis 19 reveals the attitude of Israel in the face of Canaanite perversions.[20]

Marriage, one's neighbour's marriage, is one of the institutions where Israel must preserve safe and sound the gift of fertility which the creator has bestowed upon man. 'You shall not commit adultery', that is, you shall not violate the marriage of another, is one of those short, lapidary sentences which have been preserved in the Ten Commandments.[21] However unaffected Old Testament faith may be when faced with physical love, it is quite inexorable in this matter. It presumes that even foreign potentates are aware that this is a boundary which none can cross.[22] The Old Testament never makes light of an existing marriage or of adultery, as does the world of today.

The Old Testament knows nothing of a command which prescribes only one marriage. Like neighbouring cultures it admits quite ingenuously the possibility of several marriages. Ezekiel 23 narrates the allegory of the two women whom Yahweh took to himself. These two women symbolize the two states of Israel. The Old Testament in this matter lives in the sociological framework of its surrounding world in that the patriarchal structure of society causes it no problem at all. The possibility exists that a man may leave his wife. But Old Testament law makes a decided attempt to protect the person concerned, in the case in point, the woman. The legislation concerning slaves in the book of the Covenant lays down that a female slave who has been taken to wife may not be sold again (Exod. 21.8). When a man repudiates his wife it is prescribed in Deuteronomy 24. 1–4 that the written note of divorce must be made out to her, so as to establish that she is free from blame.

Two further comments must be added to this picture of the Old Testament's quite unencumbered relationship to the world in the area of 'be fruitful and increase'. First: the 'be fruitful and increase' is a divine blessing which was pronounced over the creature man. It is the attitude of the Old Testament that a blessing always remains a free gift of God and never becomes something to which he is obliged. The world, which bears within itself all that is required for fertility, can never cut itself free from its creator and stand over against him as an independent, self-contained cosmos. The Old Testament writers know quite well that fertility remains a promise. In the case of those childless women of whom the Old Testament speaks, the only way open is the way of prayer and patience. This is the case both in the story of Abraham and in the narrative of Hanna. It can also happen that God may demand that the blessing he has given be returned to him, as is clear in the Elohist's narrative of the sacrifice of Isaac. The introductory verse tells that God is testing Abraham (Gen. 22.1). There is also the story of Job. The faith which quite simply accepts the worldly gifts of fertility and increase must always remain conscious that these blessings are a gift, and not a right. Such openness to the gifts of the world is, in the attitude of the Old Testament, the only correct way of understanding its relationship to the world.

Secondly, the Old Testament shows that where there is a blessing there can also be the danger of temptation and collapse, when man forgets the giver of the gift and makes himself the lord. We have spoken in the previous chapter of such a darkening of a world which has been blessed, and of the caricature presented by a world in revolt. Genesis 3 has something to say about this to the world of today.

'... in labour you shall bear children'. These are Yahweh's words to the woman who with her husband has forfeited her place near to God (Gen. 3.16). The joy of the blessing, bearing children, is now tied to the burden of pain, which extends beyond the case of childbearing into the whole world. And in the same breath Yahweh says something of the relationship between man and woman which is so joyfully praised in the Song of Songs: 'You shall be eager for your husband, and he shall be your master.' The reference here is to the distortion which can occur in marriage, when the woman who longs for her husband finds him to be a

38   *The Old Testament and the World*

tyrant. And it must be remarked that tyranny and servile dependence have established their rule far beyond the realm of married life.

The distortions which God's blessings can undergo extend beyond the phenomena mentioned in Genesis 3 and characterize the whole world of mankind. If Genesis 3 has shown man to be the oppressor of woman, the Wisdom writings often enough portray woman as the seducer of man. Proverbs 7 paints a brilliant picture of the foolish young man who is seduced into adultery by the woman on the street and so led on to his own destruction. G. Boström has demonstrated that one can find here traces of 'peeping' Aphrodite (*parakyptousa*), the 'woman at the window', who appears in other places as Astarte.[23] Even the Preacher, whose words about enjoying life with the woman you love we have already read, has these dark words to say about woman:

> The wiles of a woman I find mightier than death; her heart is a trap to catch you and her arms are fetters. . . . I have found one man in a thousand worth the name, but I have not found one woman among them all.

But he adds nevertheless a comprehensive sentence acknowledging what is in man:

> This alone I have found, that God, when he made man, made him straightforward, but man invents endless subtleties of his own (Eccles. 7.26–9).

There are other accounts which demonstrate the extraordinary and ever-increasing power that sin acquires when proper order in respect of marriage is rejected. David violates the marriage of his soldier Uriah and sins with his wife Bathsheba. The author of the succession narrative goes on at once to describe how David's eldest son Amnon, seized with passion, offends against his half-sister Tamar, with the consequent hate and murder within the family of David.[24] God's blessing can become so ambiguous in the hands of man. In the face of such distortions does not the call to turn from the world and its 'be fruitful and increase' have perhaps a more valid right?

On the contrary, it cannot but impress that the Old Testament, in spite of such ambiguity and fragility which is built into the relationship between man and woman, never takes this way out.

Neither in respect to the path which man must tread, nor to the goal to which he knows that this path is directed, is there the slightest sign of any admonition to turn from the blessing which God has given to the world.

The Old Testament is a book that reveals a consciousness of both hope and the future.[25] What God gave to the world with his blessing at creation recurs again in these pictures of hope. In Ezekiel 36.11 Yahweh makes a proclamation for the time when the devastated mountains of Israel will be built upon again: 'I will plant many men and beasts upon you; they shall increase and be fruitful.'[26] Jeremiah 23.3 speaks of the time when Yahweh's flocks will be gathered together again in the land: 'And they shall be fruitful and increase' (cf. Jer. 3.16). And the promise to those who observe the prescriptions of the law of holiness, which closes the book of Leviticus, runs: 'I will look upon you with favour, I will make you fruitful and increase your numbers: I will give my covenant with you its full effect' (Lev. 26.9). Just as at the beginning of creation there is no sign of any ascetical withdrawal from the world which God has graciously blessed, so too there is no sign of it as the perspective closes. According to Jeremiah 33.11, when the devastated city of Jerusalem is restored: 'In this place shall be heard once again sounds of joy and gladness, the voice of the bridegroom and the bride; here too shall be heard voices shouting, "Praise the Lord of Hosts, for he is good, for his love endures for ever".'[27]

He who has been saved will one day thank God for his blessing.

4

... AND SUBDUE IT

God's blessing upon man in Genesis 1.28: 'Be fruitful and increase, and fill the earth', is followed immediately by the words, 'and subdue it'. This command is made specific: 'Rule over the fish in the sea, the birds of heaven, and every living thing that moves upon the earth.' These words of blessing, which describe the consequences of man's likeness to God, re-echo God's introductory reflection which preceded the actual creation of man: 'Let us make man in our image and likeness to rule the fish in the sea, the birds of heaven, the cattle, all wild animals on earth, and all reptiles that crawl upon the earth' (Gen. 1.26).

What was said of the blessing conferring fertility can be repeated here: it is a blessing which bestows an extraordinary richness, a richness which goes far beyond the first blessing. The first blessing embraced man and the animal world together and conferred on man, as well as on the animals, the power to beget new life. Now man is elevated above the animal world and marked with a special dignity which derives from his likeness to God.[1] Recent discussion of the meaning of 'the image of God' makes it likely that its background is the god-like image of the king in the neighbouring countries. This idea is now, as it were, democratized—the way to this had already been prepared in Egypt—and transferred in a quite general way to man. He must subdue the earth and rule over the whole animal kingdom.

Psalm 8 catches man's sense of awe at this privilege within the world of creation, though one must not overlook the fact that the praise is directed exclusively to Yahweh, the creator. The opening and closing verses form, as it were, a frame which resumes the theme of the Psalm: 'O Lord sovereign, how glorious is thy name in all the earth!' The following verses speak of the firmament

which God has founded, and the word 'earth' carries the full force
of 'world', which embraces heaven and earth. In the shadow of the
lofty praise given to Yahweh, man is once again the subject:

> When I look up at thy heavens, the work of thy fingers,
> the moon and stars set in their place by thee,
> what is man that thou shouldst remember him,
> mortal man that thou shouldst care for him?
> Yet thou hast made him little less than a god,[2]
> crowning him with glory and honour.
> Thou makest him master over all thy creatures;
> thou hast put everything under his feet:
> all sheep and oxen, all the wild beasts,
> the birds in the air and the fish in the sea,
> and all that moves along the paths of ocean.[3]

Man's privilege of dominion is spoken of in a spirit of complete awe.

It will be useful here to look more closely at what the priestly
writer has had to say about this privilege. What has already been
said in praise of the goodness of creation is repeated. The priestly
writer is aware that there is a shadow falling across the light of the
world of creation. The early chapters of Genesis speak of the food
which is to sustain man and the animals. The green plants of the
field are assigned to the animals; in addition to these, there is
assigned to man fruits of the trees, but *not* the flesh of animals.
One can sense that behind this allotment of nourishment there lies
hidden the belief of the priestly writer that it was part of the
original disposition of the world that man does not kill the
animals. Genesis 9 offers proof that this interpretation is not a
false lead. It is the priestly account of the ordering of the world
after the flood which, according to 6.11, came about because
violence and corruption had begun to spread over the earth. The
world after the flood is no longer the world before the flood. This
is clear from God's introductory words to the family of Noah
which had been saved. He repeats the blessing of creation: 'Be
fruitful and increase, and fill the earth.' Then there follows
immediately:

> The fear and dread of you shall fall upon all wild animals on earth, on
> all birds of heaven, on everything that moves upon the ground and all
> fish in the sea; they are given into your hands. Every creature that
> lives and moves shall be food for you; I give you them all, as once I
> gave you all green plants.

But there are two restrictions: under no circumstances is man to partake of the blood of the animals he has been permitted to slaughter. As man allows the blood to flow away each time he slaughters an animal, he is to remember that in this period after the flood, where so much has become dark, man is no longer simply the master of old.[4] And secondly, human blood is never to be shed.

> He that sheds the blood of a man,
> for that man his blood shall be shed.

So runs the ancient legal prescription of Genesis 9.6, which is in the polished form of a chiasmus, each part comprising three words. The priestly writer is also aware of the dark shadow of fear which the dominion of man spreads over the lower creatures, that discord to which the Yahwistic writer draws attention with the example of the enmity between man and the serpent (Gen. 3.15). It is part of the prophetic expectation of peace that one day harmony will be restored between man and beast, so that the infant shall play over the hole of the cobra (Isa. 11.6–8).

But these shadows which, in the period after the flood, lie over the power assigned to man, should not obscure the fact that this power was promised him in the context of a blessing.

The blessing, it must be noted, is in the imperative. What is a privilege is at the same time a command; it is God's will sending man into the world and making him part of it. Man is not called to withdraw diffidently from the world; he is sent into it with a commission. 'All is yours': these words of Paul (1 Cor. 3.22) are in the best Old Testament tradition. Man is called then to make use of the world.

The Old Testament writers of course have no idea at all of modern means of mastering the world. They know nothing of scientific research which penetrates the secrets of every area of life, nor of technology which puts these discoveries to practical use and turns them into a means of easing the burdens of life. The attention of Genesis 1 and Psalm 8 is directed primarily to trapping fish, birds, and beasts and making use of the flocks. The text offers no further reflection on what hunting and fishing could mean for an epoch in which men had no use for the spoils of the hunt or the catch and did not kill animals. As hunter and shepherd man is exercising a part of that authority over the world which has been conferred upon him.

But in the Old Testament there is a still more subtle way of exercising power over the world. We must look now at what is known as 'Wisdom', which is represented by a not inconsiderable body of writing.[5]

It has become clear today that Wisdom is a phenomenon which reaches far beyond the boundaries of Israel. We are familiar with an abundance of Wisdom texts from Egypt as well as from Mesopotamia.[6] The Old Testament Wisdom literature harmonizes well with the beginning of Genesis: what is peculiarly Israelite retreats into the background in favour of what concerns man as such (analogous to the corresponding literature in the surrounding world), while in Genesis it is not a question of subduing the world of Israel, but the world which man inhabits.

Curiosity after knowledge is the beginning of the subjection of the world. And the beginning of knowledge is the naming, the fitting of what is observed into human speech. Yahweh leads the animals before the man to see by experiment if there is a helper among them suitable for him; the man names them and at the same time co-ordinates them; and he shows by the sort of name that he gives to each that there is no helper suitable for him—it is quite different in the case of the creature whom he calls wo-man, from man, *'ishshah* from *'ish*. This is the first sign of an attempt to dispose the world in the language of man. Herder insisted on the use of this text in his treatment of the origin of language.[7]

This joy in naming as one of the first acts of understanding, and the consequent enumeration of what has been understood, has its counterpart in the Wisdom literature of Israel's neighbours in what are called the Onomastika.[8] Many such are known to us from Mesopotamia. Though the intention of putting in order the various written characters may well have given the first impulse to record such series of names, there was later added the further intention of gathering together the things of the world in a definitive order and context. The outcome was that there developed in the series *Hubullu* a canonical form consisting of twenty-four tablets and thousands of names.[9] Fragments of this have been discovered at Ugarit in North Syria. The purpose of the encyclopaedic collection of the things of the world becomes quite clear in the introduction to the great Wisdom list of the Onomastikon of Amen-em-opet of Egypt from about 1100 B.C. It begins with the title:

The beginning of teaching about . . . everything that is, that Ptah has created and Toth has recorded, about the heavens and what belongs to it, about the earth and what is in it, about what the mountains sprout forth and what the floods water, about everything of which Re sheds his light, and about all that grows on the earth.[10]

Then there follow in the text which has come down to us 610 entries, a more or less orderly classification of what pertains to man and the world outside him. Albrecht Alt has proposed the attractive thesis that there is a reference to such lists in the Old Testament in 1 Kings 5.12ff. (English version 1 Kings 4.32ff.). It is said there of Solomon that 'he uttered 3,000 proverbs, and his songs numbered 1,005. He discoursed of trees, from the cedar of Lebanon down to the marjoram that grows out of the wall, of beasts and birds, of reptiles and fishes'. One would like to see behind this an indication of a quite artistic collection of sayings and poems about nature which follows the lines of the Onomastika. One could set beside this the quite vivid enumeration of the phenomena of nature in God's speeches in Job 38ff. which reflects a very careful observation of nature.[11] And finally S. Herrmann has asked whether in Genesis 1, with its orderly enumeration of plants and animals, we might not recognize the use of one of these Wisdom catalogues.[12]

The sayings of the book of Proverbs 30 have preserved for us certain observations about nature which go beyond mere enumeration. The principle of classification here is different. It is much more that of material content. One can recognize readily the riddle or the simple catechetical device of question and answer:

Four things there are which are smallest on earth
yet wise beyond the wisest:
ants, a people with no strength,
yet they prepare their store of food in the summer;
rock-badgers, a feeble folk,
yet they make their home among the rocks;
locusts, which have no king,
yet they all sally forth in detachments;
the lizard, which can be grasped in the hand,
yet is found in the palaces of kings (Prov. 30.24–8).

In another place man is the object of observation. Here the introduction is more highly developed. Two successive numbers are

mentioned, the second of which would have been originally an or-
dinal number, but has now become a cardinal:

> Three things there are which are stately in their stride,
> four which are stately as they move:
> the lion, a hero among beasts,
> which will not turn tail for anyone;
> the strutting cock and the he-goat;
> and a king going forth to lead his army (Prov. 30.29–31).[13]

The last word of the text is unfortunately not quite certain. But
one can sense in this last line a gentle undercurrent of irony, just as
in the first comparison one experiences a sense of awe. This awe is
clearly expressed in another passage:

> Three things there are which are too wonderful for me,
> four which I do not understand:
> the way of a vulture in the sky,
> the way of a serpent on the rock,
> the way of a ship out at sea,
> and the way of a man with a girl (Prov. 30.18–19).

Awe can be mingled with a sense of mystery as, for example, in the
passage which, after a not altogether perspicuous introduction,
proceeds:

> Three things there are which will never be satisfied,
> four which never say, 'Enough!'
> The grave and a barren womb,
> a land thirsty for water
> and fire that never says, 'Enough!' (Prov. 30.15–16).

The observations about nature in the divine speeches in Job all
point to something awesome, not accessible to human understanding. So man, as he restlessly questions the mystery of nature, is
confronted with a divine order which surpasses his understanding. The limits of what man can do as he sets out to subdue the
world are here clearly laid down.

But Wisdom is concerned not merely with the incomprehensible, with what is above man. She is concerned too with what is
accessible, with what is very close at hand. Such wisdom is in the
foreground both in the book of Proverbs and in the book of
Ecclesiastes. In the Old Testament the craftsman, who is an
expert in his work, can be classed among the wise. So, too, people
like Bezzalel, whom Moses commissioned to build the tent of the

meeting (Exod. 31.1; 35.30). Those women too are wise who are skilled in weaving the material for the holy place (Exod. 35.25). This manual competence is also regarded as a gift from God as, for example, the cleverness of the farmer who knows the laws that govern farming, which Isaiah 28.23–9 lists in detail in his parable of the farmer. During the course of the year he uses different instruments; he ploughs, scatters, sows: 'Does not his God instruct him and train him aright?' And the description of the different ways in which the produce of the harvest is treated, closes with the words: 'This message, too, comes from the Lord of Hosts, whose purposes are wonderful and his power [Wisdom] great.'

The key word 'counsel' describes a characteristic aspect of Wisdom. Wisdom proves itself in counsel. This touches the area of political decision. The ingenious narrative of the succession to David's throne describes in 2 Samuel 17.1–14 the scene in which the fate of the revolution is decided as a struggle between two counsellors. Absalom loses both the throne and his own life because he follows bad advice—in accordance with the mysterious will of Yahweh, says the narrator. Not only in the realm of politics, but also in everyday life it is important to take good advice, to know the way the world functions, if life is to go on successfully. In this manner one can see how a knowledge of what goes on in the world of nature can be the source of pertinent advice for man's practical life:

> Go to the ant, you sluggard,
> watch her ways and get wisdom.
> She has no overseer,
> no governor or ruler;
> but in summer she prepares her store of food
> and lays in her supplies at harvest.
> How long, you sluggard, will you lie abed?
> When will you rouse yourself from sleep? (Prov. 6.6–9).

This small representative of the animal kingdom can be a model for proper order in the life of man.

The word 'order' is a key word which has gained great significance in the more recent research into the Wisdom literature. Attention has been drawn to the importance of the word *Maat* in Egyptian literature. The word is usually translated by 'truth' or 'right'. According to H. Gese the most appropriate translation is 'world order'.[14] It describes alike the order of the external world and the order of the life of man. It is in this context that one should understand those admonitions of Egyptian wisdom which urge man to have complete confidence in this order even when it is beyond his comprehension.

The wisdom of the biblical proverbs is not far removed from this mentality. In the latest collection in the book of Proverbs 1–9, the idea that Yahweh has created the world in wisdom often appears. Proverbs 8.22ff. personifies Wisdom as she speaks in the first person before the event of creation:

> The Lord created me the beginning of his works,
> before all else that he made, long ago.
> Alone, I was fashioned in times long past,
> at the beginning, long before earth itself.
> When there was yet no ocean I was born,
> no springs brimming with water.
> Before the mountains were settled in their place,
> long before the hills I was born,
> . . .
> when he prescribed its limits for the sea,
> and knit together earth's foundations.
> Then I was at his side each day,
> his darling and delight,
> playing in his presence continually,
> playing on the earth, when he had finished it,
> while my delight was in mankind.

Christa Kayatz in her studies on Proverbs 1–9 has observed that Wisdom is described here in terms very like those used to describe the creator god Atum in Egyptian literature.[15] Maat is also described here as a child that stands before the god. The affectionate relationship of Atum to his child is noted. In another place it is said of the sun god: 'Ra has created Maat, he cried with joy over her. He takes his pleasure in her, he loves her, his heart is happy when he sees her.'[16] It is likely that we are dealing here with a direct influence on Israel of the Egyptian wisdom concerning Maat, though this cannot be readily demonstrated.

Belief in an established order in which the wise man takes his place is to be seen too in the sayings about the life of the individual and in the admonitions which direct it. It is a rule of life that 'idle hands make a man poor; busy hands grow rich' (Prov. 10.4). The wise man accordingly will also be industrious. On the other hand it is just as certain that 'ill-gotten wealth brings no profit; uprightness is a safeguard against death' (10.2). The order, that the doing of right leads to life and the doing of wrong leads to death, has quite a special place in the wisdom of Proverbs. 'Wise' and 'just' have accordingly become synonymous in this context. Many proverbs speak no longer of the wise, but of the just or of the unjust. The faith of Israel, which is familiar with the justifying will of Yahweh, has made an unmistakable impression on Old Testament wisdom and thereby made its own contribution to the Wisdom literature of the Ancient Near East.

Klaus Koch, in an article which has attracted much attention,[17] has proposed the thesis that in the Old Testament one must come to terms with the tight inner cohesion between what is done and its consequences; one is embedded in the other and we can no longer speak of retribution by Yahweh. This connection, he thinks, is something taken for granted by the Wisdom mentality. It is a distinguishing mark of the world which confronts the wise man.

The question must be raised here whether we are faced with a phenomenon which, though different in form, has marked points of contact with the concept of the cosmos in the Greek world: belief in a world which operates according to its own rules of order, in which Yahweh would merely take over the function of guaranteeing this order which is quite comprehensible in and of itself. Man, put into this world, could of his own ingenuity find his way about quite well in the order which is there; he could, by and large, include Yahweh in his plans as a factor, a quite superior one, in this order.

It is quite clear from the creation narratives and their praise of the divine order that they take no account of a world self-contained in its own system of laws; on the contrary, everything is related directly to Yahweh and his will. Should the view of the world of the Wisdom literature be so different?

Closer examination shows that the wisdom of Proverbs has something quite different to say. Scattered through the more ancient collections there are many sayings which speak quite clearly of Yahweh's freedom, which does not take its stand on man's planning. 'Man plans his journey by his own wit, but it is the Lord who guides his steps' (16.9). 'A horse may be ready for the day of battle, but victory comes from the Lord' (21.31). Reference can also be made, as in these two Proverbs, to the place where the authoritative decisions are made—one thinks here of the history of the succession to the throne of David; it is Yahweh who finally and freely determines what is to happen: 'The king's heart is under the Lord's hand; like runnels of water, he turns it wherever he will' (21.1). God reserves the final decision to himself; it allows no adaptation to any human plan, however ingenious. Proverbs 21.30 expresses this decisively: 'Face to face with the Lord, wisdom, understanding, counsel go for nothing.'

What has been said reveals Wisdom's own attempt to inquire into the order into which the divine plan has put man. It is an attempt to come to terms securely with the order of the world, which man wants to understand, and to make room for Yahweh as a factor in the order of the world. One senses quite readily in Proverbs the awareness of the danger of excessive self-conceit and of security in one's knowledge:

> Put all your trust in the Lord
> and do not rely on your own understanding.
> Think of him in all your ways,
> and he will smooth your path.
> Do not think how wise you are,
> but fear the Lord and turn from evil.
> Let that be the medicine to keep you in health,
> the liniment for your limbs (Prov. 3.5–8).

There echoes here the basic theme of all Wisdom's admonitions, which is expressed so concisely at the beginning of the first collection: 'The fear of the Lord is the beginning of knowledge' (Prov. 1.7).[18] This is in opposition to any attempt to grasp for knowledge of the order of the world as the man in the garden of paradise grasped for the fruit which promised to give him the knowledge of good and evil.

It is significant for the Old Testament that this admonition does not remain on the general level. There are in the canon of the Old Testament two books which, each in its own peculiar way and with its own emphasis, attempt to define the proper understanding of 'the fear of Yahweh'. The first is that of the Preacher, Qoheleth (Ecclesiastes).[19] He is one of those whose wisdom has allowed him to go out into the world with the confident belief that life can be mastered. There appear everywhere in his sayings elements of wisdom which are found as well in the book of Proverbs. 'The wise man has his eyes in his head, but the fool walks in the dark' (2.14). 'The fool folds his arms and wastes away' (4.5). 'Wisdom makes the wise man stronger than the ten rulers of a city' (7.19). 'The man who digs a pit may fall into it . . .' (10.8).

Throughout one can see how Qoheleth confronts the uncontrollable. He also takes a look at nature, but this is only marginal to his thinking. His gaze is not open to the wonder and beauty of the world before whose order the wise man stands in awe and from which, as in the observation on the ant and its industry, he draws conclusions for himself for his own conduct. We encounter a wise man who is in fear before the mysterious course of nature and who must regard it as a movement inaccessible to man, subject to an intransigent law.

> The sun rises and the sun goes down; back it returns to its place and rises there again. The wind blows south, the wind blows north, round and round it goes and returns full circle. All streams run into the sea, yet the sea never overflows; back to the place from which the streams ran they return to run again (1.5–7).

It is difficult to see in these words a description of a cycle of nature constantly recurring according to a fixed law, by which one would suddenly arrive at a quite negatively orientated view of the world, which could regard the cosmos apart from God. Rather is he trying to express how tightly closed the external world remains to any attempt of man to grasp it.

It is quite clear where Qoheleth's own constantly repeated reflections on the world lie: in the realm of man. He is fascinated by the mystery of the passage of time into whose hidden order man cannot penetrate. This is made impressively clear in the seven balanced couplets which begin with the very significant reflection on being born and dying:

> For everything its season, and for every activity under heaven its time:
> a time to be born and a time to die;
> a time to plant and a time to uproot;
> a time to kill and a time to heal . . . (3.1ff.).

This monotonous succession finally issues in the summary reflection: 'I have seen the business that God has given men to keep

them busy. He has made everything to suit its time; moreover he
has given men a sense of time past and future, but no comprehension of God's work from beginning to end.' So everything that, according to the wisdom and order of the wise, seems to be so ready
to hand, escapes man. It can happen that a man works in-
dustriously and then derives nothing from his industry. It can
happen that a man is just and then has to suffer the fate of one
whom God has abandoned. It can happen that a man has wisdom
and by his sage political advice could save a city which is besieged
by the enemy; but the city is lost, because unfortunately he is poor
and no one heeds his advice. 'Dead flies make the perfumer's
sweet ointment turn rancid and ferment' (10.1).

We might think that Qoheleth, in the light of these experiences,
would have to come to the conclusion that he must flee from this
world—whether this flight be to withdraw into himself or into
scepticism. But strangely enough neither the one nor the other occurs. When faced with the question of the meaning of the mystery
of the passage of time which in its movement is incomprehensible
to man, he answers: 'I know that whatever God does lasts for
ever; to add to it or subtract from it is impossible. And he has done
it all in such a way that men must feel awe in his presence' (3.14).
There is here set down definitively what true Old Testament faith
must never forget, that the world in its every detail is completely
dependent on the God before whom man must live in reverence.
With this is connected another genuine Old Testament conviction, that man, without any illusion that he will become master of
the secrets and the wisdom of the world, nevertheless must reach
out for the good things that God has given him and enjoy them in
the midst of this world which he cannot comprehend: 'I know that
there is nothing good for man except to be happy and live the best
life he can while he is alive. Moreover, that a man should eat and
drink and enjoy himself, in return for all his labours, is a gift of
God' (3.12–13).

The whole of Qoheleth is a unique critical confrontation with a
wisdom which wants to be the master of life and to be able to lay
the foundation of a lasting dominion over the world. It is a very
strong reminder that the commission, 'Subdue it', refers to the
world over which God rules, and never to a cosmos in which man
could establish himself with what he had shaped, in something, as
it were, which he had secured as his own.

The muted debate which runs through Qoheleth comes into the open in the heart of the book of Job. The form is very different; it concerns an individual and a just man who has been stricken beyond endurance; he debates with his friends who are pious, wise men. They are the vehement defenders of God whom they think they understand. Their categorized thought patterns reveal their own dominating fixations. They become ever more firmly entrenched as they continue their discussions with their suffering friend, whom they have come to console, convinced that Job must have been a sinner if such a calamity has befallen him. On the other hand, Job, in all his passionate grappling with the incomprehensible with which he has been stricken, remains the defender of the incomprehensibility of God. He insists that God must reveal him as innocent; and he establishes thereby that the rigid attitude of his pious friends, who imagine that they can control the world, is false and dishonest. In his appeal to the witness, whom he knows to be above him in heaven, and to the redeemer and avenger who will acknowledge him after his death (19.25), he reveres God more uprightly than do his friends with all their apparent piety. Certainly Job is reprimanded for his unruly disputatiousness in the divine speeches in which his attention is directed by God to all the mysteries which are locked up in the world and to God's supremacy as creator. At the same time, however, it is made clear in the hearing of his friends that he has spoken more uprightly than they.

In all the dark night of the soul which he suffers, Job shows no sign of withdrawing in any way from the world or from its riddles. He must stand firm in his suffering and not explain it away. At the same time the book makes clear that the involvement in the world, with which man has been charged, and the subjection of the world to which man has been called, has always to do with the world over which God alone is the Lord.

The creation account formulated God's command as 'Subdue it'. Qoheleth and Job are the unimpeachable witnesses that every act of subjection of the world, every act of dominion over it, is a gift from the hand of him who always and alone remains the Lord.

With full knowledge of this Lord and with the reservation that he always keeps the last word for himself, the Old Testament makes its demand for subjection of the world and for courage to face this task.

5

THE PEOPLE AND ITS ENEMIES

We have pursued in the last three chapters those lines of thought concerning man's relationship to the world which follow from the creation narratives of Genesis 1ff. We must now recall what was established in the first chapter: Israel's faith, and consequently her further reflection on man's place in the world, is a result of an encounter with Yahweh which was experienced by the group that came out of Egypt and whose confession of faith ultimately constituted the twelve tribes. It is in the liberation from the slavery of Egypt that Israel becomes conscious of God's approval of her right to live as God's people. It is this word of approval that helps her to understand what she is; and it is with this knowledge that she campaigns against those who attack her life. And life in the world, especially the history of a group of people, is never without attack or without enemies.

We see how a very early attack, which reaches right back into the desert period, has engraved itself deeply in the consciousness of Israel. Exodus 17.8–16 tells that the desert tribe of the Amalekites attacked the group which came out of Egypt, even before it reached Palestine, at a place called Rephidim, which we can no longer localize.[1] In this context 'the Lord said to Moses, "Record this in writing, and tell it to Joshua in these words: I am resolved to blot out all memory of Amalek from under heaven".' Moses built an altar and called it 'the banner of Yahweh'. And he said: 'Lay hold of the banner of Yahweh! Yahweh is at war with Amalek from age to age!' (Jerusalem Bible).[2] This event and its inheritance have quite notable effects in the later history of Israel. In 1 Samuel 15 Saul is commissioned by Samuel to campaign against Amalek and to put him under the ban. Saul did not carry out his commission fully, notably by not laying everything under the ban;

and this, according to the narrative, was the cause of the breach between him and Samuel. The last historical information that we have of campaigns against the Amalekites occurs in the narrative of the rise to power of David. During the period in which David lived in the city of Ziklag as a henchman of the Philistines, he made two campaigns against the Amalekites (1 Sam. 27.8; 30.1ff.). And further, at the end of the legal section of the book of Deuteronomy, we read:

> Remember what the Amalekites did to you on your way out of Egypt, how they met you on the road when you were faint and weary and cut off your rear, which was lagging behind exhausted: they showed no fear of God. When the Lord your God gives you peace from your enemies on every side, in the land which he is giving you to occupy as your patrimony, you shall not fail to blot out the memory of the Amalekites from under heaven (Deut. 25.17–19).

No other people that was an enemy of Israel has been so threatened with utter destruction as the Amalekites; yet this would have been of but marginal significance for Israel as a political unit when she later settled in the land. It seems to be something of a persistent afterglow of an early searing experience; of an attack on the existence of those who had just been saved from Egypt, a rejection of them in the very act of Yahweh's approval. This could well explain the words of Deuteronomy: 'Do not forget it.' Amalek had made himself an enemy of Yahweh in opposing those coming out of Egypt. Therefore: 'Lay hold of the banner of Yahweh.'

Later, Israel had no lack of enemies. The historical value of the account of the conquest of the land west of the Jordan in the book of Joshua is questionable. The conquest of Jericho is narrated in Joshua 6. The archaeological excavations at Jericho seem to indicate that the city was not inhabited at the time when those who came from Egypt entered the land.[3] Joshua 8 gives an account of the taking of Ai. The word *ha 'ai* is the usual Old Testament name for a ruin. The city then is nothing but an abandoned heap of ruins whose real name was no longer known.[4] One comes across sounder historical recollections in the account of the battle at Gibeon (Josh. 10), where a fragment of ancient song is quoted. It seems that here Israel joined forces in an alliance with four Canaanite cities against another group of Canaanite cities. It is not clear what is being reported in Joshua 11 about the conquest of Hazor in the north. If the studies of Albrecht Alt are correct, then it would seem that the settlement of the twelve tribes in the land was a much more peaceful process than the book of Joshua indicates.[5] The tribes would have established themselves mainly on the as yet uninhabited mountain range, have avoided any confrontation with the cities in the plains and on the range, so far as there were any on the latter, and have entered into friendly alliances with some cities, such as the four around Gibeon.

On the other hand, the accounts in the book of Judges of the battles with those people who were already settled in the land rest on a much sounder historical tradition. There are battles against different opponents. The story of Deborah in Judges 4 recalls the battle at Gibeon. The occasion was that the tribes of Issachar and Zebulun on the edge of the plain of Jezreel had come under the domination of the Canaanite states into whose domains they had ventured. At the spirited initiative of a woman, Deborah, a group under the leadership of Barak of the tribe of Naphtali assembled, and succeeded in overthrowing the Canaanites and their war chariots. The Canaanite leader Sisera of Harosheth-of-the-Gentiles, a city on the western end of the plain of Jezreel, fled and was disposed of at the hand of a woman from a nomad group of Kenites. The victory song of Judges 5 which, in contrast to the song at the battle of Gibeon, is preserved in its entirety gives a very good idea of the impression which the victory made on Israel.

The tribes which settled in Gilead in east Jordan and the Benjaminites who occupied an area west of the Jordan, had experiences of a different kind. They were oppressed by the Ammonites and Moabites, both related by blood to Israel. In the case of the Moabites (Judg. 3), it was a daring individual, Ehud, who stabbed the enemy king in his own palace and set in motion the freedom movement among the Benjaminites. In the case of the Ammonites (Judg. 11), it was Jephthah, duly appointed leader of the army on a contractual basis, who won freedom.

Different again was the kind of oppression caused by the mobile hordes of camel nomads from Midian. They used to appear at harvest time like a swarm of locusts, ravage the crop, and disappear as quickly. It was Gideon of the tribe of Manasseh who delivered the final blow that kept them for ever out of the land of Israel (Judg. 6–8).

Finally, mention must be made of the Philistines. In the context of the great migrations of the sea peoples, and at about the same time as the Israelites left Egypt, they occupied the coastal area of what later became Philistia. The Egyptians had great trouble in maintaining their own borders against them. Five Philistine kings, from the cities of Gaza, Ashkelon, Ashdod, Gath, and Ekron, made an alliance and exercised an ever harsher pressure on the mountain range in the interior, where they set up outposts. The stories of Samson (Judg. 13–16) are to be understood in this setting. It was only the early kingdom of Israel, first under Saul and then under David, that could supply resources to lift this oppression. It is important to realize in the context of our inquiry, which aims at understanding the attitude of Old Testament faith to the world, that it is not only the early battle against Amalek in the desert which is experienced as an action of Yahweh and consequently as part of the faith, but also the early battles in the land. 'So perish all thine enemies, O Lord; but let all who love thee be like the sun rising in strength', is the concluding wish of the song of Deborah (Judg. 5.31). This shows with all the clarity one could desire how immediately Israel's faith is related to the world. Her enemies who are defeated in this battle are Yahweh's enemies. Israel has gone out into battle, as we read in Judges 5.11, 13 as 'the people of Yahweh'—or linking it more immediately with the battle, as 'the battalion of Yahweh'. For this reason Yahweh has fought with and for his people.

> O Lord, at thy setting forth from Seir,
> when thou camest marching out of the plains of Edom,
> earth trembled; heaven quaked;
> the clouds streamed down in torrents.
> Mountains shook in fear before the Lord, the lord of Sinai,
> before the Lord, the God of Israel (Judg. 5.4–5).

Later in the poem it is mentioned that even the powers of nature took part:

> The stars fought from heaven,
> the stars in their courses fought against Sisera (v. 20).

But the city of Meroz, which did not send any troops to help in the battle, though, it would appear, obliged to do so, is cursed:[6]

> A curse on Meroz, said the angel of the Lord;
> a curse, a curse on its inhabitants,

because they brought no help to the Lord,
no help to the Lord and the fighting men (v. 23).

In 1951 Gerhard von Rad published a thin but significant monograph entitled *The Holy War in Ancient Israel*.[7] He sees in the holy war a cultic institution of ancient Israel. If one were to remain closer to the languages used in the Old Testament, one would prefer to call it the Yahweh war. Numbers 21.14ff. quotes a fragment of a song and states explicitly that it comes from 'The Book of the Wars'. It seems that there was an ancient collection of songs which dealt with 'the Wars of Yahweh'.[8] Unfortunately we have no information about the relationship of this book to 'The Book of the Upright' from which the fragment quoted in Joshua 10.13 comes, as does also, according to 2 Samuel 1.18, the lament of David over Saul and Jonathan; nor do we know if the song of Deborah comes from one of these books.

It must not be overlooked, and von Rad has rightly insisted on this, that the wars of Yahweh are spoken of in a highly stylized form in the Old Testament. Each description of a war does not contain every detail. But when all the details are drawn together then we have, according to von Rad, something like the following. The call to Yahweh's war comes through a blast on the trumpet—Saul's call to war in 1 Samuel 11.7 is quite unusual; in a fit of anger he carves up a pair of oxen and sends the pieces through all Israel with the oath that the same would be done to the oxen of any man who did not follow him into battle.[9] The assembled army of Yahweh is under strict instructions to maintain the ritual purity of the camp. After sacrifice and consulting God the charismatic leader proclaims: 'Yahweh has given the enemy into your hands.' The army marches out in the certainty that Yahweh is with it and that its enemies are no longer merely the enemies of Israel, but the enemies of Yahweh. The people is admonished not to be afraid. It can then happen that terror in the face of Yahweh strikes the enemy so that they are drained of courage. Israel advances against its enemies with the battle cry, *teru'ah*;[10] the enemy are terrified in the presence of Yahweh and are incapable of real opposition; and as is related in the battle of Gibeon, they turn their swords against each other in confusion. The song of Deborah shows that one can even speak of the immediate intervention of Yahweh who makes use of the powers of nature which are at his disposal. This is clearly the experience in the battle that Deborah directed when a great rainstorm rendered the battlewagons of the Canaanite kings incapable of functioning. The older texts speak of an actual battle between men; the song of Deborah strikes the daring note that the people of Meroz should have come to the assistance of Yahweh; the later texts emphasize Yahweh's action much more strongly and allow human activity to recede to the background. The descriptions of the battles of Yahweh reach their climax in the books of Chronicles where Yahweh alone is the one who fights. But this is already present in the description of the battle against the Philistines under Samuel in 1 Samuel 7: Samuel offered a sacrifice at Mizpah; Yahweh then thundered over the armies of the Philistines so that they took to flight and nothing remained for the Israelites but to pursue them. After the victory has been won the ban is carried out: the whole of the booty is set aside for Yahweh and there is a renunciation of any private enrichment, this being expressed in the annihilation of everything alive.

To what period of Israel's military campaigning is this description of Yahweh's war most suited? The answer would point to the battles in the period before the formation of the state which are described in the book of Judges and in the beginning of the first book of Samuel. There is no state system here which obliges the king to defend the people against the enemy. The stories of the individual judges, however different they may be in detail, show that in a time of dire emergency men arose who took the leadership in hand, gathered the people around them into an army, and knew how to become master of the situation. Generally speaking, no fixed pattern for acquiring lasting leadership had been worked out. The wars of that time were not wars of conquest. Rather were they defensive wars, whose purpose was to bring fresh security and freedom to tribes who were oppressed. Israel saw in these wars, just as she had seen in Egypt, Yahweh's approval of her freedom of life, and her enemies as the enemies of the divine will.

The whole event of the conquest of the land is now seen in retrospect as filling out the pattern of Yahweh's war, which ran its course with a ban on the population of the conquered area. In the design of the book of Joshua the migration into the land takes on a bloody character which historically does not belong to it.

Ultimately all praise must be given to Yahweh who by his power gave the land to the people. We must deal with the meaning of the land in the following chapter.

Actually the exercise of the ban had already begun to fall into disuse in the early period of the monarchy. The account of King Ahab's war against Syria in 1 Kings 20 shows that there were hard-line prophetic groups which insisted on its being carried out, while the king himself had no thought at all of putting to death King Ben-hadad of Damascus whom he had taken prisoner. Some of the laws of Deuteronomy too indicate that there was a real effort to humanize war. The address which, according to Deuteronomy 20.2–4, one of the priests was to give to the army before going into battle, shows again and quite impressively the unsophisticated directness with which Israel regards the struggle for her position in the world as Yahweh's business. The priest says: 'Hear, O Israel, this day you are joining battle with the enemy; do not lose heart, or be afraid, or give way to panic in face of them; for the Lord your God will go with you to fight your enemy for you and give you the victory.'

In the pre-monarchical period and at the beginning of David's time the ark of the Covenant was carried into battle as a sign of Yahweh's presence in war. The history of the ark, this object of cult which holy legend derived from Moses, and something of its fate, as narrated in Jerusalem, is told in 1 Samuel 4–6 and 2 Samuel 6. This history can uncover an earlier period and a quite different aspect of Israel's faith in 'Yahweh's war'.[11]

1 Samuel 4 tells that the Israelites, who had been defeated in battle by the Philistines, brought the ark from Shiloh down to the battle line in the firm belief that the victory must be theirs. But it turned out that not only were they a second time unsuccessful in battle, but also the sacred pledge of the divine presence fell into the hands of the Philistines and was carried away by them as part of the booty. It is not necessary here to trace further the extraordinary history of the ark, which finally returned to Israel and was transferred by David with great ceremony to Jerusalem. It is sufficient in the present context to establish the freedom of Yahweh which will be clearly affirmed in the history of Israel's defeat. Yahweh remains the master of his decisions. He does not owe Israel victory. That will be maintained here.

Something is revealed here which will emerge ever more clearly in the course of Old Testament history. One could first of all establish from a purely historical point of view that the form of the Yahweh war begins to disappear from the beginning of the monarchical period. One could add then that the institutionalized monarchy shows less and less the characteristics of charismatic leadership. Even under David there had begun a phase of foreign conquest which could only with difficulty be brought within the framework of belief in Yahweh who secures Israel's existence.

But alone this is not a sufficient explanation. More and more there prevails the conviction of Yahweh's freedom. For all that he is bound to Israel, and however much his concern for Israel remains, every one of Israel's wars cannot be simply called a war of Yahweh nor every enemy of Israel Yahweh's enemy. The great prophets are the men who proclaim this freedom. Something more must be said of them in this context.

But the movement is already there in the stories about the earlier prophets. In 1 Kings 19.15ff., Elijah, who has fled from Ahab and Jezebel to God's mountain, Horeb, receives from Yahweh the commission:

> Go back by way of the wilderness of Damascus, enter the city and anoint Hazael to be king of Aram; anoint Jehu son of Nimshi to be king of Israel, and Elisha son of Shaphat of Abel-meholah to be prophet in your place. Anyone who escapes the sword of Hazael Jehu will slay, and anyone who escapes the sword of Jehu Elisha will slay.

The narrative breaks off after a few verses; later (2 Kings 8.7ff.), it is narrated how Elisha went to Damascus and there promised Hazael that he would be king of Aram. The episode in which this takes place moves to an extraordinary climax:

> The man of God stood there with set face like a man stunned, until he could bear it no longer; then he wept.[12] 'Why do you weep, my lord?' said Hazael. He answered, 'Because I know the harm you will do to the Israelites: you will set their fortresses on fire and put their young men to the sword; you will dash their children to the ground and you will rip open their pregnant women.

Hazael will do all this as God's gruesome instrument, because of Israel's sinfulness. The man who, according to the rules of the Yahweh war, would be called an enemy of Yahweh, is here the instrument of the holy God, the judge and helper of Yahweh.

What is here but a distant beginning emerges incomparably

fuller in the proclamation of the great writing prophets. Amos, the first stormy petrel, who began his work at a time which was apparently quite peaceful and prosperous, can speak of a coming deportation of the people to an exile beyond Damascus (Amos 5.27). He does not indicate any concrete political enemy. This man from the Judean countryside sees drought, plagues of locusts, earthquakes as the special dispensers of Yahweh's judgement. The scene is the same with Hosea. The Assyrians have burst into Syria, and people run off to Egypt for help and fawn on the whim of the eastern king. Hosea can say that the image of the calf-god honoured in the cult at Bethel will be carried off to Assyria as tribute to the great king (10.6), and that Israel must return into Egypt (8.13). Yahweh himself is at work in the enemy which threatens Israel. 'But I am a festering sore to Ephraim, a canker to the house of Judah ... yes indeed, I will be fierce as a panther to Ephraim, fierce as a lion to Judah—I will maul the prey and go, carry it off beyond hope of rescue—I, the Lord' (5.12, 14). Who is Israel's enemy here? Hosea's shocking message is that Yahweh himself is the enemy.

It is advisable to stay a little longer with the prophet Isaiah. It is in Isaiah that Yahweh's freedom comes clearly to the fore. He has spoken his approval to Israel in the course of her own history, and he goes together with his people in the course of the history of the world, without allowing himself to be enmeshed in any historical system. Isaiah likes to describe Yahweh as 'the Holy One of Israel'. One can sense in the background echoes of Isaiah's experience when he was called in the temple of Jerusalem and heard the seraphim singing the Trisagion. The phrase, the Holy One of Israel, includes at the same time two things: the knowledge of Yahweh's readiness to show real concern for Israel; and the freedom of the Holy One, who can become a consuming brand to his people and who in any case continually confronts his creature with his holiness.

Isaiah, like his predecessors among the writing prophets, is summoned to proclaim over Judah the imminent judgement. In his early proclamation in 2.12ff., he speaks of the mighty 'day of Yahweh', a theme which carries traces of Amos, a day on which everything on high will break upon the earth.[13] He sees a fearful people bursting into the land from afar off (5.26ff.), a people to whom no opposition can be offered.

In the year 733 the storm clouds began to gather over Judah.[14] The two neighbouring kingdoms in the north, Syria-Damascus and North Israel, had united so as to force Judah into an anti-Assyrian coalition. They took into their army a candidate for the throne of Jerusalem, a son of Tabeel, of whom nothing more is known. It seems that Isaiah saw in this event the fulfilment of the judgement which he had long since pronounced over Judah. But instead of this, something else took place. It is reported in 7.1ff. that King Ahaz had apparently gone to inspect the city's water supply; Isaiah met him outside the city and addressed him: 'Be on your guard, keep calm; do not be frightened or unmanned by these two smouldering stumps of firewood ... this shall not happen now, and never shall.' Why this surprising and unconditional promise of support together with the admonition not to be afraid?

Perhaps something may be said by way of explanation: Isaiah's message becomes much clearer in what follows. It has its origin in the form of a promise of salvation by the Holy One of Israel to his people which is quite peculiar to Jerusalem. It is not the old promise of Exodus that is the central point here; it is the promise of 2 Samuel 7 where Yahweh, through the prophet Nathan, spoke to David and his house, and assured him as king of Israel's future. When the two northern kings come and arrogantly include in their army a candidate for the throne who is most probably not of the Davidic line, do they intend thereby to do violence to God's historical plan? On this occasion they are the enemies of Yahweh because they are setting themselves over and above his promise.[15] Isaiah's word, like the war speech of Deuteronomy 20, urges confidence and trust.

But does Yahweh take his place in the front line of his people as the ancient formulas of the Yahweh war believed? Isaiah's address to Ahaz concludes with a brief and brilliant word-play: 'Have firm faith, or you will not stand firm.'[16] One is not going too far in seeing behind this episode the intention, or even measures already taken by Ahaz, to make himself safe against the enemy from the north with the help of Assyria. The account in 2 Kings 16.7–9 of Ahaz' subsequent conduct makes this quite probable. Isaiah's message of deliverance from this imminent threat calls on Ahaz to have the courage to rely on the help of the Holy One of Israel, who will abide by his promise.

This becomes even clearer in the subsequent exchange with

Ahaz. Isaiah quite boldly offers Ahaz a sign on behalf of Yahweh that would confirm the surety of his promise. But Ahaz rejects it with a pious-sounding phrase: 'I will not put the Lord to the test by asking for a sign.'[17] Clearly he will not commit himself. Isaiah indignantly takes up the reply: 'Listen, house of David. Are you not content to wear out men's patience? Must you also wear out the patience of my God?' The difficult question as to how Isaiah's sign, the immediate birth of a child, Immanuel, is to be understood, cannot be treated here. This at any rate seems clear, that as Isaiah develops his reply to Ahaz he mingles together in a quite unusual way both a promise of salvation and a promise of destruction:

> Before that child has learnt to reject evil and choose good [i.e. shows the first signs of using his judgement], desolation will come upon the land before whose two kings you cower now. The Lord will bring on you, your people, and your house, a time the like of which has not been seen since Ephraim broke away from Judah.[18]

What then will be the course of this divine attitude of friend and foe? Yahweh remains completely free in that the two aggressors from the north will vanish like a ghost. At the same time, however, there is a proclamation of judgement which threatens Judah and its royal house:

> On that day the Lord will whistle for the fly from the distant streams of Egypt and for the bee from Assyria. They shall all come and settle in the precipitous ravines and in the clefts of the rock; camel-thorn and stinkwood shall be black with them.

The land of Judah will become the battleground of the great powers. The following oracle (7.20) speaks even more sharply: 'On that day the Lord shall shave the head and body with a razor hired on the banks of the Euphrates, and it shall remove the beard as well.' The Assyrian will burst into the land of Judah as an enemy and as an instrument of Yahweh and will complete his work of destruction.

Assyria then has become in reality the fate of Palestine. North Israel and Aram-Damascus have been destroyed under its attacks. The rabble of soldiery has raged mercilessly. Isaiah 9.4–5 gives some hint of the harshness of the military boot and of the blood that flowed from its rough-shod tramp.

The oracles of Isaiah 10.5ff. and 14.24–7 show that Yahweh is no debtor to the Assyrian power. Assyria too will be brought before Yahweh's judgement, because it wanted to be more than an instrument and allocated to itself complete power.

What Isaiah could but outline in a few bold strokes should have made clear how little Yahweh allows himself to be drawn to support any front, even in this most stormy period when the prophets spoke. At the same time this proclamation makes clear how decisively the faith of Israel is confirmed by Yahweh's freedom in the process of history, and how the people is involved in the decisions taken.

Old Testament faith and its relationship to the world is involved in what is said here about Israel and her enemies. Yahweh has not called his people to a withdrawal from history and the world; he confronted it and made it his people in the midst of history. In response to this call the people conducted its wars as Yahweh's wars, and Yahweh's approval is seen where he has sent the people one who is to save it from its enemies. The message of the prophets makes it even clearer that while Yahweh does not dispense his people from the world of historical experience, he does not just allow himself to be used in any historical movement. Jeremiah and Ezekiel can demonstrate how Yahweh can carry out his work of judgement on his people in the one who destroys Jerusalem. Yahweh, through Jeremiah 25.9; 27.6; 43.10, calls this destroyer 'Nebuchadnezzar my servant'; not only the military leaders of Judah, but also those prophets of victory who opposed Jeremiah, thought that they could call a holy war against him in Yahweh's name. It would be left to Deutero-Isaiah to show how in the period of blackest night Yahweh, in a way quite beyond expectation and for many of the pious exiles quite beyond belief, deals with Israel and speaks his concern to his all but defunct people. His instrument is the Persian prince Cyrus whom, through Isaiah, he addresses with the title of 'my anointed' (45.1).

This faith, bound to the events of history, is not experiencing the moodiness of a God who, without rhyme or reason, today says yes and tomorrow no. Israel experiences in all this the God who in his holiness is leading his people; he says yes to his people and no to their enemies; he will lead them to where they will forget any claim of their own, and teach them to live only by the gift which has been given them. He is leading them to the discovery that their most dangerous enemy is their own revolt against God.

This historical confrontation with earthly enemies is also 'the world', the place where Israel is called to believe and is spoken to in God's action. It is not that history carries within itself its own self-sufficiency and presents an enclosed system of truth. Rather it is the prophetic word sounding over the events of history that, by virtue of God's power, makes history speak.

This becomes clear in a type of literary speech which is characteristic of the prophet Ezekiel.[19] Exclusive to Ezekiel and occurring constantly throughout is the literary form of 'proof-text'. Certain historical proclamations, as well as proclamations of judgement before the disaster of the year 587 and oracles against foreign peoples, often gather into the concluding sentence: 'And they shall know that I am Yahweh.' The purpose of this literary form is to stress that every action of God, be it judgement or justification, has as its object to make Yahweh known to his people and beyond them, as is expressly stated in some places, to the nations. Just as in former times the Exodus from Egypt made Yahweh known to his people through his interpreter Moses, so now Yahweh's action of judgement and justification in history, which the prophet proclaims, makes him known. This then by way of summary: there is not in the Old Testament any Stoic severance from the external world and its vexations or any withdrawal into the indifference of a self-sufficient, peaceful impassivity (*ataraxia*). The enemy, and vulnerability in the face of the enemy, are in the Old Testament always an utter reality. And that is to be seen not merely where the people stand confronted by their external enemies. It is quite clear too in the Psalms, where it is the individual who is attacked by his foes. It has always caused a great deal of head-shaking and aroused some derogatory observations that in a Psalm like Psalm 23, 'The Lord is my shepherd', which is so alive with trust in Yahweh, the enemy suddenly appears: 'Thou spreadest a table for me in the sight of my enemies.' But is not the Old Testament, with its constant watchfulness against attack, which is never a matter of indifference but must be undergone, the true pathfinder to the gospel of the New Testament? The demand, 'Love your enemies',[20] certainly occurs in the Old Testament; yet it is not at the very centre of belief as it is in the New Testament, where faith has its origin from the proclamation of the crucified. But can this proclamation be heard at all where a man has withdrawn from vulnerability to attack by retreat into the realm of Stoicism? Indifference, which is far removed from hate and love alike, because it has turned its back on the world, will never be able to comprehend what the cross proclaims and what the prophetic message of the Old Testament is leading to: that God, in his initiative of grace, is calling to himself in the judgement of the Calvary event, a world which has become his enemy. To be able to be God's people, the people to whom he has addressed his acceptance, when we must with all justice be addressed as his enemy, that is the context, that the depth of trial, out of which we can fully understand what it is to love our enemies.

The Old Testament is ever bringing to the fore that God, even when he appears to oppose his own people as their enemy and it is impossible to see where he is leading them, is always acting as one concerned for his people. This compassionate concern which with utter gratuity calls God's people to himself and promises that no opposition, not even the gates of hell, will overcome it, is ultimately the deepest source of the call, 'Love your enemies' (Matt. 5.44). Because 'the love I speak of is not our love for God, but the love he showed to us . . .' (1 John 4.10).

6

LAND AND POSSESSION

In his little book *Israel and Palestine* Martin Buber gives a citation from Moses Hess, who was originally a close associate of Karl Marx, but later separated from him because of his Zionistic attitude. Moses Hess, whom his contemporaries derided as the communist rabbi, wrote:

> The first commandment of God which he as the creator of all races has planted in our hearts, and which is the source and basis of all others, is that we have the commission to teach the other nations. The greatest punishment which has been laid upon us for departing from the path which divine providence laid down for us, the punishment which most weighs us down, is that we, since we have lost the land, can no longer serve God as a nation through our institutions, which could not be continued and developed in the Dispersion, because they presume a community living in the land given to our ancestors. Yes, it is the land that we lack in order to exercise our religion.[1]

This paragraph without doubt expresses genuine Old Testament tradition. Israel of the Old Testament, believing Israel, is unthinkable without this quite worldly phenomenon of the land.

For Old Testament faith the land is more than just any piece of property which one without more ado could exchange for something else, like gold or jewellery. It is a defined piece of property over which there shines the light of God's promise. On the other hand it is also quite clear that Old Testament faith learns from this defined piece of property, how to deal properly with worldly possessions. We must discuss the relationship of Old Testament faith to this area of worldly possession.

The significance of the land for Israel can be seen quite clearly early in the Old Testament where the people of Israel is just begin-

67

ning to take shape.[2] The introduction to the Yahwistic history of
the patriarchs in Genesis 12.1 tells that Yahweh addressed
Abraham and ordered him: 'Leave your own country, your
kinsmen, and your father's house, and go to a country that I will
show you.' Abraham accordingly set out and came to the land of
Canaan. The key word 'land' (country) occurs twice in this introduction. The command is that Abraham should leave
definitively the land which is his home. He must leave the land and
everything that he possesses in the land, and set out—though not
without goal or purpose. A new land is mentioned, but not named;
it is simply said that God will show it to him. And there is no misunderstanding the intention to give this land and all that is in it to
Abraham. In contrast to the land where Abraham was born and
lived, his natural home with its natural rights of ownership, this
land is God's gift to him; he is shown it and led to it.

The rest of the story of Abraham shows that this reference to
the two lands is not merely incidental and without consequence
for what follows. The land out of which Abraham was led is ever
present as the story proceeds. One knows moreover that
Abraham's natural roots, his family and family property were
there. It is to this land that Abraham's servant goes to look for a
bride for Isaac (Gen. 24). It is there that Jacob flees and brings
back his two wives, Leah and Rachel. When the servant is sent to
the land, it is impressed upon him most forcefully that Abraham's
son is not to be brought back there. And in the case of Jacob it is
taken for granted that he will return again to Canaan. One must
not lose sight of what is being said: it is not what Abraham has in-
herited by natural right from his parents that is in reality to be his
property. He is cut off decisively from this property. He must
learn to see his property in a quite different perspective.

This aspect is further stressed in a quite surprising way in what
follows. Abraham is not just given property in the land to which
God has led him, as one might expect. He remains for a time a
long way from being a property holder. He must wait, ever
moving towards a future not yet given to him. He is a guest, an
alien among those to whom the land belongs.

It is the latest strand of the priestly tradition that underlines
this and gives it its own orientation. The Fathers live as *gerim*,
'strangers', or to translate the word more accurately, as 'aliens', in
the land to which they do not belong, i.e. as people who as yet have

no rights in the land and consequently cannot own property.

The only breach of this rule appears to be in Genesis 23, where the priestly tradition narrates a story quite peculiar to it, whose main, though hidden, theme is the question of the possession of the land. Abraham's wife Sarah has died. Should Abraham bury her in land which is the property of the Canaanites, her, the ancestress of the chosen people, which one day is to take possession of this land? There follows a rather detailed story in which there is no mention of God.[3] In an apparently quite worldly business deal Abraham manages to buy from the inhabitants of Hebron a small piece of land with a cave where he buries Sarah. The purpose of details, with the drawn out, cunning haggling about the value of the field, is to ensure beyond any doubt the right of possession of this piece of land. But what has Abraham gained of the promised land? Merely a field with a burial chamber. All that he possesses in the land is a grave, to all appearances the confirmation of transitoriness, but in this case an unmistakable sign of the promise of the future. This is an extraordinary way in which to express expectation of a promise for the future which has not been redeemed.

This long expectation of the Fathers leans clearly towards a coming fulfilment. At the very beginning, just after Abraham has arrived in the land, the Yahwist narrates that Yahweh appeared to him at Shechem and promised: 'I give this land to your descendants' (Gen. 12.7). In the following chapter Abraham's nephew Lot appears to have chosen the best part of the land for himself. Yahweh spoke to Abraham again:

> Raise your eyes and look into the distance from the place where you are, north and south, east and west. All the land you can see I will give to you and to your descendants for ever. I will make your descendants countless as the dust of the earth; if anyone could count the dust upon the ground, then he could count your descendants. Now go through the length and breadth of the land, for I give it to you.

It has been remarked that one of the rites involved in taking possession of a piece of property was to walk across or around it.[4] According to David Daube,[5] gazing across the property was a form of taking possession. So Abraham was to walk through the length and breadth of the land, carrying out so to speak in anticipation the rite of taking possession of the land which he was *"restless wandering" also from God to God.*

still waiting to be presented to him.[6] The restless wanderings of the semi-nomads would be explained by a quite peculiar transformation of its meaning as a rite of first possession.

The depth of Israel's reflection on the mystery of why God keeps the bearer of the promise so long in a state of suspense becomes clear from Genesis 15.16. It is a subsequent development of the scene of the covenant which Yahweh struck with Abraham at night. Verses 13–15 look at Israel's stay in Egypt and speak of the long period that the nation which descends from Abraham must wait; they will remain, as it were, in an ante-room, in humiliating slavery, in a land that does not belong to them. It then continues: 'And the fourth generation shall return here, for the Amorites will not be ripe for punishment till then.' The question about the reason for the long wait is answered by a reference to God's justifying action. God is just in regard to the Amorites, the former possessors of the land. But the sinfulness of these inhabitants is not yet such that God could take the land from them and hand it over to new owners.

The time is ripe when the people are led out of Egypt. It is not necessary to illustrate at length the joy with which the Old Testament writers speak of the beauty of the land which has been given to Israel. One citation from the introductory sermons of Deuteronomy will suffice:

> The land which you are entering to occupy is not like the land of Egypt from which you have come, where, after sowing your seed, you irrigated it by foot like a vegetable garden. But the land into which you are crossing to occupy is a land of mountains and valleys watered by the rain of heaven. It is a land which the Lord your God tends and on which his eye rests from year's end to year's end (Deut. 11.10–11).

This is an echo of earlier eulogies of the land. There is the much older description that speaks of 'the land flowing with milk and honey'. And there is the phrase attested in Jeremiah,[7] which has become a code word for the promised land in Daniel,[8] namely 'the land of the fairest', or simply 'the fairest'. There is no limit to the joy which describes the land which God gave Israel as her possession.

One would like to ask if, besides this boundless praise of the land to the people, there are not more reserved voices which would have a qualifying effect.[9] One could refer to three groups of texts.

There are the Rechabites, who derive from Jehonadab, son of Rechab, and who are mentioned in 2 Kings 10.15ff. They were like-minded contemporaries of Jehu at the time of his revolt against the royal house of Ahab and Omri, and the context indicates that he, Jehonadab, was particularly zealous for the Yahweh faith. The group of Rechabites who descend from him appear in a later context in Jeremiah 35. Jeremiah invited them to take some wine, but their spokesman replied:

We will not drink wine, for our forefather Jonadab son of Rechab laid this command on us: 'You shall never drink wine, neither you nor your children. You shall not build houses or sow seeds or plant vineyards; you shall have none of these things. Instead, you shall remain tent-dwellers all your lives, so that you may live long in the land where you are sojourners.'

There can be no doubt that the Rechabites are a group who are determined in their zeal for Yahweh; in contrast to the marked tendency to follow Canaanite customs under the Omri dynasty,[10] they have sharply rejected the produce of the land, especially the fruit of the vine—and this is characteristic of them—as well as any settled homestead in the land. This is not a rejection of the land, as if one would have to leave it and go out into the desert again. The words of their spokesman make this clear. It is a deeply religious rejection of certain sociological structures and property practices. It would be an error too to speak of any idea of poverty, inasmuch as the group most certainly possessed flocks. It is rather something of a return to an earlier sociological stage, basically that of the patriarchs, and therefore a measure, historically founded, by which it is intended to be particularly pleasing and obedient to Yahweh. And there is no indication at all that the group was of the opinion that the whole of Israel would have to return to such a way of life. Even Jeremiah, who holds the group up as a model to Israel because of its special fidelity to the instructions of their ancestors, does not propose their way of life as that which is demanded of the whole of Israel. He quite unconcernedly offers the Rechabites wine. But more than this, it is related that during the siege of Jerusalem he made use of a right of redemption which he had to buy a field in Anathoth on behalf of a relative. And the message of Yahweh came to him out of this context: 'For these are the words of the Lord of Hosts, the God of Israel: the time will

come when houses, fields, and vineyards will again be bought and
sold in this land' (32.15). The building of houses and the laying out
of vineyards were part of the picture of promise which Jeremiah
offered the people as judgement threatened.

The second group which might be mentioned are the Levites,
whom the law would not allow to possess land. A. H. J. Gunneweg
speaks of 'the Levite rule'.[11] Whatever might be the answer to the
difficult question of the origin of the Levites, it is clear that the
tribe of Levi had no territory of its own when the twelve tribes
were settled, and the status of the individual Levite corresponded
sociologically to that of a tent-dweller without land. Here, as in
the case of the Rechabites, there is no indication at all that this
should be the status of all Israelites. It is rather a question of a
special status among the people, sanctioned by Yahweh, and
enjoying its own privileges, according to Deuteronomy, whose
opinion it is that all priests should be Levites:

> The levitical priests, the whole tribe of Levi, shall have no holding or
> patrimony in Israel; they shall eat the food-offerings of the Lord,
> their patrimony. They shall have no patrimony among their fellow-
> countrymen; the Lord is their patrimony, as he promised them
> (Deut. 18.1–2).

The existence of Levi ought not to make its patrimony an object
of suspicion to the rest of Israel.

The prophecy of Hosea is the third source from which it was
thought possible to establish a nomadic ideal.[12] There is no mistaking that Hosea looked back into the desert period as the time
when Israel was still fully committed to her God:

> But I have been the Lord your God since your days in Egypt,
> when you knew no other saviour than me,
> no god but me.
> I cared for you in the wilderness,
> in a land of burning heat, as if you were in pasture.
> So they were filled,
> and, being filled, grew proud;
> and so they forgot me (Hos. 13.4–6).

In his message for the future he says: 'But now listen, I will woo
her, I will go with her into the wilderness and comfort her' (2.14).
But he continues immediately:

There I will restore her vineyards,
turning the Vale of Trouble into the Gate of Hope,
and there she will answer as in her youth,
when she came up out of Egypt (2.15).

The passage through the desert is but a transitory phase of her education. The goal remains life in the land. Hosea pinpoints here very clearly the greater danger of the possession of the land and, more than this, the danger of any possession at all: 'When she became sated, then her heart became proud, and so she forgot me.' Possession threatens to wipe out the memory of the giver and leads to the diabolical temptation through which all can be lost as the event of the exile makes quite clear.

The Old Testament then looks at the land in which Israel lives and pronounces complete approval. Yahweh does not want a people that is poor and without land. He does want a people that always acknowledges him as the Lord and Giver-over and expresses this in its practical life.

It is well to refer in this context to the way in which the land was divided up in the book of Joshua. The division of the land begins in chapter 13. Joshua casts lots 'before Yahweh' (18.6), to see which part of the land each tribe is to get. This means that even when it comes to details it is Yahweh who assigns to each tribe what section of the land it will possess. It is a matter of dispute how much of this represents a genuine memory. Albrecht Alt is of the opinion that we probably should not completely exclude the religious aspect from the division of the land among the tribes.[13] In any case this is the pattern according to which a later era thinks of, and comes to terms with, the possession of the land. It is narrated in 1 Kings 21 that King Ahab wanted very much to buy a vineyard which was near his palace, so as to make a garden out of it. He offered the owner Naboth something in exchange or its value in silver. But Naboth rejected the offer with these words: 'The Lord forbid that I should let you have land which has always been in my family.' This is more than mere peasant conservatism. It is the reaction of an Israelite who regards his land as a gift given to him by God, that cannot without further ado be exchanged or sold.

The advance of money as the medium of exchange and of commerce could not be halted in later times. In the eighth century, however, we hear the passionate protest of two prophets against such activity: 'Shame on you! You who add house to house and join field to field, until not an acre remains, and you are left to dwell alone in the land' (Isa. 5.8). It is a revolt against Yahweh, whose will it is that everyone should have his own section of the land, while individuals set about making themselves great landowners. The prophet Micah sees the fate of the poor man and says:

> Shame on those who lie in bed planning evil and wicked deeds
> and rise at daybreak to do them,
> knowing that they have the power!
> They covet land and take it by force;
> if they want a house they seize it;
> they rob a man of his home
> and steal every man's inheritance.
> Therefore these are the words of the Lord:
> Listen, for this whole brood I am planning disaster ... (2.1–3).

Albrecht Alt has supported the thesis that the critically emended continuation of this verse directed against the great landlords who lived in Jerusalem, threatens a new division of the land in which the oppressed owners will have their rights restored.[14] However this may be, a sharp polemic is pronounced here against the great landowners who take no account of God's will in respect to the land. 'One man, one house, one plot of land', such is Alt's formulation of the ancient and holy instruction of Yahweh.[15]

A word is in order here about the proposed division of the land in the outline of the end of time in Ezekiel 48. The new proposal, in the form of a priestly statute, is contrasted with the disorder of the pre-exilic period. It is most unlikely that the plan came from the prophet himself; more probably it came from the school that gave the book its final form. The plan is to be understood as the counterpart of the division of the land under Joshua.[16] It presumes, as G. Macholz has underlined, a free peasant social structure and the old tribal system of Israel.[17] What is really new in this plan is that the land is not just divided into twelve parts according to the number of the tribes (Joseph is divided into Ephraim and Manasseh, while Levi drops out); there are thirteen parts. There is a special strip in the centre of the land which is to be known as the *terumah*, the reserve. The temple stands there; the priests and Levites live round about it; there is a section for the city—Jerusalem is not named—and for the prince. The temple is the real centre of this area. The land is portrayed as a sacred offering, the best part of which is reserved for God, while the people receive their duly assigned portions from the remainder, which is schematically divided into twelve strips. The land is considered to be a gift through which the giver is honoured by some part of it being given in return.

We must now turn to Leviticus 25 which, with its laws about the sabbath year and the jubilee year, is of such significance for the understanding of the land and its possession in the Old Testament.[18] Leviticus 25.1–7 deals with the sabbath year. Every seventh year is to be a sabbath for Yahweh, i.e. the land is to lie fallow. There is to be neither sowing nor harvest. Ancient customs, originally concerned with the mysterious powers of the earth and its being allowed to lie fallow, are referred here to Yahweh. The untilled land is 'a sabbath to the Lord'. Just as Ezekiel 48 acknowledges the real owner of the land by setting apart and consecrating a thirteenth division from what is assigned to the tribes, so too the unploughed land of the sabbatical year keeps alive the memory of the true owner of the arable land. It is quite significant to see how the ancient law of the book of the Covenant develops further the prescription for the sabbath year:

> For six years you may sow your land and gather its produce; but in the seventh year you shall let it lie fallow and leave it alone. It shall provide food for the poor of your people, and what they leave the wild animals may eat (Exod. 23.11).

The demand to renounce the harvest for Yahweh's sake turns attention automatically to the poor who are neighbours. This aspect of Old Testament thought will be treated in the next chapter but one.

The description of the sabbath year turns one's attention in yet another direction. The period of inactivity at the end of seven days is also described as the sabbath. The Israelite, by observing this period of abstention, which persevered much more strongly than the sabbath year, acknowledges the Lord of time in the gift of time. The renunciation of the use of time every seventh day is done for Yahweh's sake and acknowledges him as the Lord of time.[19] The greedy grasping after all time, after every single day, which will be used for merely human gain, is rejected. Possession of time like the possession of land is a possession which is a gift.

We must here make a brief reference to the command to free the Hebrew slave every seventh year, a command which likewise occurs in the book of the Covenant. A similar command is found in the Code of Hammurabi, but with a different lapse of time.[20] Inasmuch as the seventh year is introduced here, this demand to make a free gift of a possession is to be seen in the light of a free gift for Yahweh.

A further development of the instructions for the sabbath year, found in Deuteronomy, is instructive. During the monarchy simple agricultural exchange and exchange in kind began to give way to exchange by money. It is significant that the system of fallow and release did not remain fossilized in ancient forms. Deuteronomy 15.1ff. shows a change in the matter of the remission of debts: 'At the end of every seventh year you shall make a remission of debts.' This important sentence refers originally to the land lying fallow. It has been rendered quite differently in today's context by the following legal interpretation:

> In face of the damage caused by the early capitalistic period, the institution of the sabbath year is extended here to arrangements for debts, which had secured the giving of a loan by personal arrest. In the year of remission the believing Israelite is not permitted to lay hold of the debtor, that is to carry out the consequences of the arrangement (F. Horst).[21]

The right which Yahweh reserves to himself prevails even in an altered system of economy.

Leviticus 25.8ff. gives the instructions for the year of jubilee, which is to be held every seven times seven years. The acknowledgement that Yahweh is the Lord of the gift, and that it is his will that the gift be properly divided, is fully institutionalized. In this year liberation is to be proclaimed through the whole land. There are two matters at issue: 'Every man of you shall return to his patrimony, every man to his family' (25.10). These two directions seem to correspond to the seven-yearly provisions just mentioned for the Hebrew slave. These directions are not developed any further, nor are they framed in any regulation. On the other hand the regulation about the reversion of property which has been sold is described in more detail and appraised in its effects on the sale of land. The basic prescription occurs in Leviticus 25.23: 'No land shall be sold outright, because the land is mine, and you are coming into it as aliens and settlers.' Those who belong to Israel are, so to speak, called back to the status of the patriarchs who, while they waited patiently for the coming of the promise, lived as aliens in a foreign land. But now it is no more the Canaanite population which is named as the lord of the land,[22] but the Lord, whom Israel acknowledges as the only Lord. Israel lived in the land of this Lord with the status of settlers.

The further prescriptions of Leviticus 25 about the lapse of rights and the prohibition of interest cannot be gone into here.

It is time now to present a synthesis of the attitude of the Old Testament to the land and its possession. The attitude to possession has been discussed rather extensively already in the context of the aftermath of the actual possession of the land.

It has become very clear from what has been said how decisively 'worldly' the Old Testament is in its attitude to the land. The opinion of Moses Hess, quoted at the beginning of the chapter, has found complete endorsement in the light of both the regulations of Leviticus 25 and the institutions which provide for the proper treatment of the land.

The land in Old Testament faith is not something indifferent that could just as well be as not be. It is something that belongs to the complete relationship of God to Israel. It is not a question of a 'blood and soil' religion, as if Israel grew up with and was bound to this soil from the very beginning. Israel is quite well aware of the contrary, namely that it is not native to this land, but has received it. The land is a gift of Yahweh, the Lord of the land, who has led Israel out of Egypt in order to bring her to the place of rest, as Deuteronomy 12.9 describes it. It acquires thereby something of a sacramental quality. It is the sign of the confirmation of God's love for Israel and of Israel's belonging to God. In her status as 'aliens and settlers' (Lev. 25.23), Israel lives in a place which is near to God, a nearness which he confirms. As long as Israel listens to the voice of her Lord, then she is doing what on her side enables her to remain near to him. This is not only an often expressed deuteronomic idea; it is linked in the Decalogue with the command to honour one's parents: 'Honour your father and your mother, as the Lord your God commanded you, so that you may live long, and that it may be well with you in the land which the Lord your God is giving you' (Exod. 20.12; Deut. 5.16).

We can understand therefore what a terrible shock it must have been for Israel to lose her land at the time of the exile, and how deeply she must have been moved by the prophetic messages of hope to turn again to the land. We have read Hosea's words. They have their quite differently formulated counterpart in Jeremiah's anticipation of the future in the purchase of the field at Anathoth. The most impressive oracles of all are those which proclaim a new Exodus from the land(s) of exile and dispersion, and which have their goal in a new entry into the land, to the 'lofty mountain of Israel', to Zion, where Yahweh is king. These occur in Exodus 20.32ff., and find their fullest expression in Deutero-Isaiah. It is quite clear in Ezekiel that it is not merely the land as such, but the land as the place where Yahweh is present. It is there that Yahweh enters into his new temple (Ezek. 43.1ff.).

This proclamation explains why Israel struggled so tenaciously, as no other people struggled, to return to her land—in the first period of exile in Babylon, and now today before our very eyes in modern Zionism, however steeped in secularity this latter may appear to be. There must be a new and quite different event to assure her of the nearness of God and to find a faith which can free it from this attachment. The New Testament, daughter of Ancient Israel, shows the conviction that this even mightier event has taken place in the Christ of Israel.

But there is something more included in what has been said: while Israel understands her land and the possession which has been guaranteed her as a gift of God's love, she is protected from making it all into an instrument of destiny to rule her faith. The land, and all that is given to Israel in the land, is more and more understood as a gift from God for which she is responsible. That sentence from Leviticus 25.23, which speaks of her alien state in this land, awakes instinctively the memory of the Pauline formula of 'having as if one had not' (1 Cor. 7.27–31). The land should not exercise a tyranny over Israel, otherwise it would no longer be the promised land of which the Old Testament speaks. Rather it has the function of both calling to mind and keeping awake the joy which can be Israel's before her God.

Israel knows that Yahweh, in giving the land, wanted to give a blessing. It would be quite easy to sketch the main lines and to show how everything good that God has guaranteed to man is understood in the context of blessing. One can proceed thence to the prescription that no one should take from another what has been given to him: 'Thou shalt not steal' (Exod. 20.15; Deut. 5.19). This command, however, envisages something quite different from the sacredness of private property—an interpretation which has often been given it in modern capitalistic society. The property that must not be taken, wife, slave, slave-girl, ox, ass, anything that belongs to the neighbour, and which a man must not allow himself to be greedy for (this is the original meaning of the word *hamad* in Exodus 20.17)[23] and which a man must not allow himself to be greedy for (this is the original ty which Yahweh has portioned out.[24] When men set about greedily carrying off and making their own what, by the will of the just one, has been justly portioned out to others, then the prophetic threat and woe sound out. The mere right of possession does not yet justify the possession of goods. The Old Testament can speak in no other way of the land or of any other property. In speaking in this way it withdraws the land and all that is in it from the cosmos, which is based on the premise that it can live within its own self-contained system. The 'world', with which the Old Testament knows that it is bound in the 'land', does not bear within itself its own dynamism; it is the world open to God and responsible before him.

7

THE PEOPLE OF YAHWEH
AND THE
WORSHIP OF YAHWEH

The illumination of Buddha, which is at the beginning of the great religious movement of Buddhism, is the experience of an individual, from whom the four great truths of life unfolded and who as a result proclaimed to his disciples the noble way of the eight stages. The history of Buddhism began with the gathering together of communities of monks, in which each individual sought to tread the way of Buddha to his own salvation just as Buddha himself had done.

Old Testament Israel acknowledges at the beginning an act of salvation which a group of people experienced, whatever may have been the way in which Moses was called to lead the group that came out of Egypt. The Israelite league, as Max Weber called the people of the twelve tribes who came together in faith in Yahweh,[1] joined itself to this confession. It was under this sign that the first change in Israel took place; it became a royal people; and after the exile in Babylon by yet a second change it became a sort of priestly church-state. What persists through all this is not the totality of a community of believers, which would be gathered by the proclamation of a founder, but rather a community whose origin is a common historical experience and which experiences even further the historical leadership of its God.

This community which came together under the name of Israel, conceived of itself right from the beginning as something different from its neighbours. We had occasion earlier to mention that ancient formula which showed how her way of life differed from that of those around: 'That is not done in Israel', and by which she describes the no less scandalous sexual excess of Canaan as 'foolishness in Israel'.[2] Both formulas expressly announce the people's ethic of Israel. The oracles of the seer Balaam, who had been brought to curse Israel but who ended by blessing her, reflects the same experience: 'I see a people that dwells alone, that has not made itself one with the nations. Who can count the host of Jacob or number the hordes of Israel?' (Num. 23.9b–10a). Israel is different from the nations. 'The nations', *goyyim*, later takes on the pejorative sense of 'heathen'. As a people, itself belonging to the world of peoples, and so very much in the world, Israel is conscious of her special place among them.

The great table of the nations of Genesis 10 tells of the 'nations' and their origin. The priestly section is quite intact, whereas the Yahwistic one is but fragmentary. We see here how mankind derives from the family of Noah which was saved in the flood; it divides into three branches, following the three sons of Noah, and so into the people of the world.

The priestly writer, with his systematic manner of presentation, emphasizes that here it is a question of the effect of the blessing which Yahweh has pronounced once more over mankind after the flood: 'Be fruitful and increase, and fill the earth.' The three great groups of nations filled the world of Genesis 10: first there are the little known descendants of Japheth in the north and in the Mediterranean; then the Hamites who, in the priestly view, occupy those areas which were under Egyptian influence before Israel became a nation, as well as Canaan;[3] and thirdly, those who derive from Shem in the east and in the north,[4] and who are closely related to Israel.[5] The priestly writer concludes with the stereotyped formula, that this is the way in which the nations developed 'by families and languages with their countries and their nations'.

It is striking that the people of Israel does not appear in this great picture of the peoples of the world. We must first of all remark that we have here traces of a genuine historical recollection that Israel is a latecomer among the nations of the world. Israel's close relations, the Edomites, the Moabites, and the Ammonites, different from the Aramaic groups, are not mentioned. And the Philistines who came into the land at about the same time as Israel are only mentioned in a gloss in the Yahwistic account, which seems to be an addition to the Caphtorites and the end of verse 14. Amos 9.7 also speaks of the Philistines as having their origin in Caphtor (Crete?).[6] The names Kerethite and Pelethite,[7] the names of Philistine battalions in the army of David, quite possibly retain traces of the name Crete.

The fact that Israel is not mentioned in the table of the nations in Genesis 10 is an indication of the feeling that the appearance of Israel was something special which cannot be properly explained by a simple genealogical tree as in the case of other nations. The same is true, though in a much lesser degree, of Ishmael, of Edom-Esau, Moab, and Ammon, whose beginning is set in the context of the beginnings of Israel.[8] It is the story of Abraham, which is concerned predominantly with the origin of Israel from promise and calling, that unfolds what is peculiar to her.

These varied passages of the Old Testament reflect the conviction that Israel is a nation demonstrably different. It would be appropriate then to raise the question of Israel's national character. The question goes back to Herder who began to inquire into the individual qualities of each race and who believed he could see them personified. This view gained great significance in the romantic period and in the nationalism that arose from it. The upsurge of national feeling, the extreme acuteness of the racial question, the rallying cry of 'blood and soil', discredited this approach during the rise of nationalism and rendered it suspect. With the disappearance of all the disease and evil thrown up in this turmoil, there remains the sober reality that nations have their own physiognomy and are characterized by definite qualities which are not just an adaptation of a broad cosmopolitanism, but which come to the fore in speech, custom, behaviour, and general attitude and consciousness. What is it that marks Israel out?

This question brings us face to face with a new aspect of our theme of the Old Testament and the world. What law is it that governs Old Testament Israel and marks her off so clearly as something so different from her neighbours? Is it some built-in law of nationalism or some sort of forerunner of later racism, when this has recourse to the peculiar nobility of its blood-line and thereby tries to maintain its racial character? The answer to this question would make clear how Israel saw herself as something special among the nations of the world, and to what peculiar variant of nationalism she saw herself obliged in this context.

One answer suggests itself. The Old Testament says, with growing emphasis, that Israel entered into nationhood with the law of Moses and has to live in accordance with it. Is the national character of Israel to be seen in the law of Moses? This is a very formal answer. It is necessary to go much more deeply into the question, into the question too of the law of Moses and what it really means. Resuming certain formulations from the beginning of our inquiry we could speak of that special directive by which Old Testament Israel was conscious of her calling to a journey and according to which she made that journey.

How did Israel identify herself under this directive? There is no lack of detailed answers to this question in the Old Testament, one of the most important of which must be singled out and considered more carefully. The account which we have of the events of Mount Sinai, to which Israel journeyed after being liberated from Egypt, reports that Moses climbed the mountain immediately after they arrived there, was addressed by God, and received a commission:

> Moses went up the mountain of God, and the Lord called to him from the mountain and said, 'Speak thus to the house of Jacob, and tell this to the sons of Israel: You have seen with your own eyes what I did to Egypt, and how I have carried you on eagles' wings and brought you here to me. If only you will now listen to me and keep my covenant, then out of all peoples you shall become my special possession; for the whole earth is mine. You shall be my kingdom of priests, my holy nation. These are the words you shall speak to the Israelites' (Exod. 19.3–6).

It is significant that this address of Yahweh which solemnly reveals Israel's destiny, begins by recalling the historical events that had just taken place. The experience of the divine action against Egypt, which gave Israel her liberty, and the consequent guidance through the desert, which is painted in the bold picture, 'I have carried you on eagles' wings', should not be left out of consideration as an unimportant preliminary when one is describing the true nature of Israel. It is the basis of what is to be said later of Israel's destiny. The song of Moses (Deut. 32.10ff.) repeats in much greater detail the image of being borne on eagles' wings, and links it in another way with the image of rescue from a desperate situation:

> He [Yahweh] found him [Israel] in a desert land,
> in a waste and howling void.
> He protected and trained him,
> he guarded him as the apple of his eye,

> as an eagle watches over its nest,
> hovers above its young,
> spreads its pinions and takes them up,
> and carries them upon its wings.

The situation in which God found his people is not described with any further detail; there is merely an indication that it was dangerous. An oracle of Ezekiel, describing the beginnings of Jerusalem, which, as the centre of Israel, represents it, goes yet a step further in its dramatic picture. It describes Jerusalem as an abandoned foundling:

> This is how you were treated at birth: when you were born, your navel-string was not tied, you were not bathed in water ready for the rubbing, you were not salted as you should have been nor wrapped in swaddling clothes. No one cared for you enough to do any of these things or, indeed, to have any pity for you; you were thrown out on the bare ground in your own filth on the day of your birth. Then I came by and saw you kicking helplessly in your own blood; I spoke to you, there in your blood, and bade you live (Ezek. 16.4–7).

This is the background, described in these three passages with ever mounting imagery:[9] Israel owes her life to her God who saved her in the face of death.

The promise of Exodus 19 takes shape before this background: 'You shall become my special possession.' It is striking that this same thought also occurs, though expressed differently, in the other two passages cited. Deuteronomy 32 makes the description of Israel as Yahweh's special possession, anticipates the saving action as the reason for it, and at the same time backdates it to the primeval period when Yahweh decided the destinies of the nations of the world:

> When the Most High parcelled out the nations,
> When he dispersed all mankind,
> he laid down the boundaries of every people
> according to the number of the sons of God;[10]
> but the Lord's share was his own people,
> Jacob was his allotted portion (Deut. 32.8–9).

Later on in the Old Testament, in the book of Daniel, we read that each nation has its own angel. The angel Michael is assigned to the people of Israel. One suspects that behind Deuteronomy 32 there is a still more ancient formula, both pre-Israelite and polytheistic, according to which the king of the pantheon assigns the nations their gods. But Deuteronomy 32 speaks much more boldly; it describes Yahweh as *Elyon*, the most high.[11] This is no accident; it is, as we have seen, the ancient Jerusalem name for the creator god; and when the nations are assigned their protecting angels, Yahweh has reserved Israel to himself. Exodus 19.5 also gives a hint of this background when it says, apparently quite illogically: '... out of all peoples you shall become my special possession; for the whole earth is mine.'

Ezekiel 16 expresses this process of 'becoming my special possession' with the even more daring picture of marriage. The foundling child that Yahweh has saved has now grown to womanhood. Yahweh passes by once again:

> Again I came by and saw that you were ripe for love. I spread the skirt of my robe over you and covered your naked body. Then I plighted my troth and entered into a covenant with you, says the Lord God, and you became mine. ... and [I] anointed you with oil. I gave you robes of brocade and sandals of stout hide; I fastened a linen girdle round you and dressed you in lawn. For jewellery I put bracelets on your arms and a chain round your neck; I gave you a nose-ring, I put pendants in your ears and a beautiful coronet on your head (Ezek. 16.8–12).[12]

Israel (Jerusalem) is conscious that she is Yahweh's special possession. Exodus 19 explains what this really means with two further details, the second of which is like what we have already been talking about: 'You are my holy nation.' The phrase 'holy nation' does not indicate primarily some lofty moral or religious quality that Israel has won for herself. It describes a quality of the people which is based on Yahweh. The holy is that which is basically reserved for God, predicated of him and belonging to him. This is the only way in which the Pauline letters speak of the holy.[13] We shall see shortly how this quality which is indicative of something in Yahweh leads to a call, to an imperative, to holiness.

The other phrase, 'You shall be my kingdom of priests', expresses the most distinguishing consequence of becoming Yahweh's special possession. The emphasis in this expression, which occurs but once in the Old Testament, is on the word 'priests'. The priest stands in the privileged place of one who has ready access to the holy and, as we often read in the Old Testament, can be near to God. His access to and nearness to God is a priestly service for others. Israel then is the kingdom of priests among peoples who have formed states and been organized into monarchies; and this might suggest that Israel too might organize herself into a constitutional monarchy. In the early post-exilic period we hear the promise once more: 'But you shall be called priests of the Lord and be named ministers of our God' (Isa. 61.6). In this vision of the reversal of the oppressive circumstances and humiliation in which the remnant of Israel lives, the hope is expressed that the nations will bring food and wealth to the priests; this idea is quite foreign to Exodus 19 which looks to the special nearness to God as the priestly privilege.

The privileges described in Exodus 19 are not just a blind stroke of good fortune that happened to Israel. The previous conditional sentence, 'If only you will now listen to me and keep my covenant (then you shall become my special possession)', makes it clear that Israel is called upon to adhere responsibly to all that God has prepared for her.

Before inquiring further into this call, another question might be placed: does not the calling to such a lofty position in which Israel sees herself evoke a quite special sense of dignity? We know from the not too distant past how a national consciousness, which is convinced of the lofty nature of the national character, immediately begins to create 'laws to protect the national honour'.

Anyone who goes through the Old Testament with this question in mind, namely, the special honour due to Israel and the instructions for the protection of this honour, will certainly come across signs of sensitivity about it. But he will search in vain for commands to protect the honour of Israel. Israel does not fit the picture of the other nations of the world who are always interested in their own honour; her honour must always and uncompromisingly retreat before the honour of Yahweh who has made her his people; she must be devoured by his honour. The contest between David and Goliath shows this quite clearly. The story of 1 Samuel 17 narrates how Israel and the Philistines were drawn up in battle order opposite each other; the Philistine giant came forward and challenged one of the Israelites to single combat. He concludes his challenge with the words: 'Here and now I defy the ranks of Israel. Give me a man . . . and we will fight it out' (v. 10). The young David, who was bringing food to his brothers in the camp, hears the men of Israel saying to each other in fear: 'Look at this man who comes out day after day to defy Israel' (v. 25). One cannot miss the difference in tone in David's excited counter-question: 'And who is he, an uncircumcised Philistine, to defy the army of the living God?' He is brought before King Saul and tells him how as a shepherd he had gone after a lion and taken the booty from its mouth. 'Lions I have killed and bears, and this uncircumcised Philistine will fare no better than they; he has defied the army of the living God. The Lord who saved me from the lion and the bear will save me from the Philistine.' And when David advanced to meet the Philistine in battle he said:

> You have come against me with sword and spear and dagger, but I have come against you in the name of the Lord of Hosts, the God of the army of Israel which you have defied. The Lord will put you into my power this day. . . . All those who are gathered here shall see that the Lord saves neither by sword nor spear; the battle is the Lord's, and he will put you all into our power (vv. 45–7).

One sees here quite clearly that defiance of Israel is experienced at once as defiance of Yahweh. Yahweh will help and will take care that this defiance is taken away.

The introductory addresses of Deuteronomy show that there has been quite a deal of reflection on the question, what precisely is Israel's special place as Yahweh's special possession, and in what does her special honour consist. The answer given to this question is very striking.

First, we hear expressed a number of rather negative disavowals whose purpose is to avoid misunderstanding. Moses recalls the acts of favour towards Israel in the gift of the land and in the passage through the desert, and rejects any thought of self-satisfaction on Israel's part:

> Nor must you say to yourselves, 'My own strength and energy have gained me this wealth', but remember the Lord your God; it is he that gives you strength to become prosperous, so fulfilling the covenant guaranteed by oath with your forefathers, as he is doing now (Deut. 8.17–18).

Even sharper is the rejection in Deuteronomy 9.4–6 when Moses refers to the conquest of those powerful people who occupied the land:

When the Lord your God drives them out before you, do not say to yourselves, 'It is because of my own merit that the Lord has brought me in to occupy this land.' It is not because of your merit or your integrity that you are entering their land to occupy it; it is because of the wickedness of these nations that the Lord your God is driving them out before you, and to fulfil the promise which the Lord made to your forefathers, Abraham, Isaac and Jacob. Know then that it is not because of any merit of yours that the Lord your God is giving you this rich land to occupy; indeed, you are a stubborn people.

This stubbornness is then further demonstrated by reference to the disobedience of the people at God's mountain, when they made for themselves a golden calf. This markedly negative quality which occurs in a book otherwise so full of the dignity of God's special possession and the holy people (Deut. 7.6; 14.2), must be taken up more fully later.

But before doing this we must look at the more positive attempts to answer the question about the special dignity of the people in the introductory addresses of Deuteronomy. This book (4.32–4) speaks of Israel's sense of her honour by referring back to the experience that she has undergone from the hand of God:

Search into days gone by, long before your time, beginning at the day when God created man on earth; search from one end of heaven to the other, and ask if any deed as mighty as this has been seen or heard. Did any people ever hear the voice of God speaking out of the fire, as you heard it, and remain alive? Or did ever a god attempt to come and take a nation for himself away from another nation, with a challenge, and with signs, portents, and wars, with a strong hand and an outstretched arm, and with great deeds of terror, as the Lord your God did for you in Egypt in the sight of you all?

This same chapter expresses quite positively what Israel's own particular dignity consists in, what is its distinguishing mark; it is there that her honour lies:

You must observe them carefully, and thereby you will display your wisdom and understanding to other peoples. When they hear about these statutes, they will say, 'What a wise and understanding people this great nation is!' What great nation has a God close at hand as the Lord our God is close to us whenever we call to him? What great nation is there whose statutes and laws are just, as is all this law which I am setting before you today? (4.6–8).

Here too the people's honour does not consist in anything which it has in itself or does, in its noble origin, its aristocratic blood, its rich territories, but exclusively in what Yahweh gave it in their encounter in history. Here, as in Exodus 19, it is quite clear that what was given to Israel was not given as an ornament to hang around its neck for purposes of show; rather, what constitutes its honour is at the same time a complete demand on it. The noble directive which distinguishes it from the nations, remains but a hollow echo if it is no more than a showpiece. It is to be carried out. Only then does it remain what it really should be.

This leads us again into a deeper question: what is the content of the command, just and good, that Yahweh has given to his people and which constitutes the wisdom and honour of Israel in the eyes of other nations? The question arises whether there is any formula in the Old Testament that draws all this together.

One must refer here to the *Shema* of Deuteronomy 6.4ff., words which once would have formed the headline of one of Deuteronomy's introductory addresses, and which right down to the present day form one of the most important parts of the Torah in the liturgical life of the synagogue. Moses speaks:

> Hear, O Israel, the Lord is our God, one Lord, and you must love the Lord your God with all your heart and soul and strength. These commandments which I give you this day are to be kept in your heart; you shall repeat them to your sons, and speak of them indoors and out of doors, when you lie down and when you rise. Bind them as a sign on the hand and wear them as a phylactery on the forehead; write them up on the door-posts of your houses and on your gates.

Yahweh, Israel's God, is One; beside him, there is no need of any other helper. This one God alone is to be loved; this is the decisive and unique part of the instruction that Yahweh gives his people, and this constitutes the honour of this people before all other nations.

Another expression of this summary form is to be found in the holiness code. The collection of commands in Leviticus 17–26 received the title of the Law of Holiness from A. Klostermann in the last century.[14] It readily prevailed. It derives from the very pregnant sentence in Leviticus 19.2 which characterizes this whole complex: 'You shall be holy, because I, the Lord your God, am holy.' The numerous and detailed instructions which cover the most diverse areas of life, and of which we shall have more to say in the next chapter, must be seen in the light of this verse. This basic formula is a quite clear interpretation of what we have read in Exodus 19: to be God's special possession, to be a kingdom of priests, and thereby to possess the privilege of special access to God, has now been turned to an imperative of the Law of Holiness which the people must carry out. Israel's honour and dignity do not consist in self-satisfied possession, but in being laid under command. The honour of this people can never consist in peacefully building up its own empire with its own wealth, but only in remaining under the call which leads it, so as to continue to be what by grace it is.

This immediately evokes one last question which, when it is a question of the honour of Yahweh's people of the Old Testament, cannot remain unformulated: is this Israel of the Old Testament that which it ought to be? This last question will have to be put to the Old Testament when we are dealing with the matter of the honour of Yahweh's people.

Among the Old Testament prophets, there is one who above all became passionately zealous for the honour and holiness of Yahweh, with which the honour and holiness of the people of Yahweh are intimately connected. It is Ezekiel. His encounter with the glory of Yahweh occurs at the beginning of his prophetic activity, in a foreign land, in the place of exile (Ezek. 1). The word *kabod*, which describes the glory, is also the word for honour.

Ezekiel dramatizes the history of Yahweh's dealing with his people in a variety of images. We have already mentioned his description of the union between Yahweh and his people under the image of the marriage bond. He is following here in the wake of Hosea. Besides chapter 16, Ezekiel uses the same imagery in chapter 23 when he describes the marriage of Yahweh with the two girls Ohola and Oholibah, whom he had rescued from Egypt and who represent the two kingdoms of Israel.[15] In chapter 20 he describes, without any further imagery, the history of Yahweh with his people whom he has rescued from Egypt. The dominant thought here is the honour of Yahweh who binds his name to his people: 'When I chose Israel, with uplifted hand I bound myself by oath to the race of Jacob and revealed myself to them in Egypt; I lifted up my hand and declared: I am the Lord your God' (v. 5). Yahweh begins by binding himself by oath to the people so that the people is known in the world as 'the people of Yahweh'. This is the honour of this people. There follows in verse 7 the binding to God's commandment. It is the beginning of a sad history between Israel and Yahweh, just as it is in Ezekiel's other historical sketches. Already in Egypt the people becomes rebellious against Yahweh's command. The disobedience continues in the desert. In each case it is only because of respect for the oath made in his name, which binds him to his people, that Yahweh withholds from the worst, the destruction of the people. Already in the desert period the decision is finally reached that Yahweh will scatter this people among the nations.

To this must be added the further details of Ezekiel 36.16ff. These verses add that the people of Israel is scattered among the nations, as was its fate in the days of Ezekiel. It is here that the history of the honour of Yahweh undergoes a peculiar development:

> When they came among those nations, they caused my holy name to be profaned wherever they came: men said of them, 'These are the people of the Lord, and it is from his land that they have come.' And I spared them for the sake of my holy name which the Israelites had profaned among the nations to whom they had gone. Therefore tell the Israelites that these are the words of the Lord God: It is not for your sake, you Israelites, that I am acting, but for the sake of my holy name, which you have profaned among the peoples where you have gone. I will hallow my great name, which has been profaned among those nations. When they see that I reveal my holiness through you, the nations will know that I am the Lord, says the Lord God. I will take you out of the nations and gather you from every land and bring you to your own soil (Ezek. 36.20–24).

There follows in Ezekiel 20.32ff. the description of the new and second Exodus from slavery, later proclaimed so joyfully by Deutero-Isaiah as imminent.[16]

This is the history of the honour of God's people as narrated by Ezekiel. It presumes that the people of Yahweh is a people among the nations, belonging utterly to the world. But when it is a question of this people's honour, then it is so very different from all that rules the nations of the world. It is the case of a people whose honour consists entirely in the mystery that the God who encountered it and dared swear his oath to it maintains his honour, which is at the same time his loyalty, despite all the disloyalty of his people. The people has really no claim to any national honour. The closing verses of chapter 20 describe what will happen when God in his favour restores his people to the land:

> There you will remember your past ways and all the wanton deeds with which you have defiled yourselves, and will loathe yourselves for all the evils you have done. You will know that I am the Lord, when I have dealt with you, O men of Israel, not as your wicked ways and your vicious deeds deserve but for the honour of my name. This is the very word of the Lord God (Ezek. 20.43–4).

These are hard words, but they are words which free God's people from stifling concern for its own honour.

In the depths of the oppression of the exile, the prophet of the exile formulates the confession which by an extraordinary transformation is alive again in the Christian community: God's people, completely in the world, called to obedience and responsibility in the world, lives exclusively from the fact of God's loyalty. The whole honour of the people, beyond which it is to look for no further honour, consists in this, that in the depths of oppression it acknowledged him, and became through his call his own special possession, his royal priesthood, and a holy people. The people of God ought to rejoice in this honour as it lives out its life in the world, and let it be the spur to confirm it daily as God's people.

The concrete manner in which God's people must live with its neighbour and in the presence of Yahweh will be the subject of the following chapter.

8

THE PEOPLE, THE NEIGHBOUR,
AND THEIR LIFE
BEFORE YAHWEH

The previous chapter was concerned with Yahweh's people and its honour. We saw that Israel's honour consisted in what was given it by its God. In particular, mention was made of the law in the Deuteronomy, which Israel had received from her God and in which she acknowledged what made her a wise and prudent people in the eyes of the nations.

We must now examine in closer detail what this means for the life of Israel. From all that has been said so far, it is to be expected that this law does not summon God's people out of the world and the world order to a life of spiritual self-perfection, but sends it out to live responsibly within itself and with the nations round about it. On the other hand the two prescriptions that stand over the book of Deuteronomy and the Law of Holiness: 'You must love the Lord your God with all your heart and soul and strength', and 'You shall be holy, because I, the Lord your God, am holy', give us to understand that Israel's relation to the world as a people of the world cannot simply be that of its neighbours. Just as Israel's honour is ultimately an utter gratuity, so must life within this people and before Yahweh be recognizable by something special.

Israel is a people among the nations. It consolidated itself in Canaan as a league in a land which was by no means bereft of inhabitants. One can surmise that not only much of the pre-Yahwistic past of the tribes made its way into the people without question, but also that much of what already belonged to the tradition of the land became part of it. This surmise is confirmed by an examination of the legal codes. In the older collection of laws known as the book of the Covenant (Exod. 20.22–3;33), there is a whole block of casuistic material (21.1—22.16) which in its precise and compact style as well as in its content stands very close to the legal codes of the great eastern and northern empires of the ancient orient.[1] The matters dealt with are the rights of slaves, killing and bodily injury, theft, damage to property, rights of deposit, rights of shepherds; it breaks off in the middle of the prescriptions about marriage. In a few places, for example in the regulations regarding killing and bodily injury, one can see in the formulation and language the influence of other regulations with regard to rights. Israel's own sense of right would have differed here from the prescriptions taken over from the surrounding Canaanite world. The death penalty for the murderer, the right of asylum for the unintentional killer and the rigid formulation of the *Lex Talionis*, which latter is found in briefer fragments and in a somewhat disturbed form in Deuteronomy 19.21 and Leviticus 24.18, 20, give indications of a different origin.

Albrecht Alt, in his thoroughgoing inquiry into the origins of Israelite law, has demonstrated that even in the more ancient non-casuistic law there are different distinctive groups which he would bring together under the title of apodictic law.[2] He was of the opinion that within this group he could set that genuine corpus of law which grew out of belief in Yahweh over against what had come from Canaan. Further discussion of the question, however, has made it clear that one has to distinguish somewhat more carefully.

To give but one example, the prohibition of Deuteronomy 19.14: 'Do not move your neighbour's boundary stone', is drawn up in the same apodictic style as the prohibitions of the Decalogue, a form which Alt regarded as characteristic of genuine Israelite apodictic style. However, in the Egyptian instruction of Amen-em-opet in chapter 6, one reads a very similar formula: 'Do not carry off the land mark at the boundaries of the arable land, nor disturb the position of the measuring-cord; be not greedy after a cubit of land, nor encroach upon the boundaries of a widow.'[3] This is the source of an instruction found in Proverbs 23.10, which is a translation of the Wisdom literature of Amen-em-opet, and which runs: 'Do not move the ancient boundary stone or encroach on the land of orphans.' It is clearly a question of an ancient prescription which is of general importance for the good order of the life of the community in these lands. It is not the instruction which is peculiar to the Old Testament, but the reason given for it, which is clear both in Deuteronomy as well as in the book of Proverbs. The complete text of the prohibition in

Deuteronomy is as follows: 'Do not remove your neighbour's boundary stone, fixed by the men of former times in the patrimony which you shall occupy in the land your God gives you for your possession.' The Israelite who has to abide by this prescription is referred not merely to the tradition of his ancestors, but also to the fact that the land in which these boundary stones were set up is a land which has been portioned out by Yahweh. One must reflect here on what has been said earlier about the land as a gift of Yahweh.[4] It is significant that the text of Proverbs, which comes directly from a translation of the Egyptian original, has also added to it a sentence which provides the motivation for not removing the ancient boundary stone or for encroaching on the land of an orphan: 'They have a powerful guardian who will take up their cause against you.' Yahweh the *go'el*, the redeemer, the guardian, enters the field in the case of the right of redemption, just as he does in the case of blood vengeance for the one who has been injured.

These reflections on one small example make us aware that in making a judgement on the Old Testament commandments one has to consider not merely the form of words of the concrete command, but also the motivation and its background. When two traditions do this, they do not do it each in the same way. The prohibition against moving a boundary stone in Deuteronomy looks to the land as God's gracious gift, which the person obeying the command must bear in mind. The formulation of Proverbs sees Yahweh as the defender of the weak and the lowly and the protector of widows and orphans.

More recently, on the basis of the similarity in form between some of the Wisdom admonitions and the apodictic commandments, even the commandments of the Decalogue, attention has been directed to tribal wisdom as a possible source of origin of such formulations. This may well be. In the case of the basic directives of the Decalogue, which were put together with the intention of covering as wide an area of life as possible, it is to be noted that they have been gathered under the great preamble in which Yahweh presents himself: 'I am the Lord your God who brought you out of Egypt, out of the land of slavery.'[5] Every individual command which is here imposed, even though it may be the repetition of a formula from ancient tribal custom, must be understood as bound to the one who deals with Israel as liberator and saviour. That region of the world, disposed according to the divine and legal prescriptions of Israel, is in any case the region where one is responsible before Yahweh, the God of Israel.

Besides this specific Old Testament motivation, to which we shall return on a number of occasions in what follows, there is something further to be remarked: namely that certain emphases in grouping together commands of similar content and notable insistence on certain areas must be regarded as peculiar to the Old Testament and different from the surrounding world.

This is particularly the case with regard to the area of justice and jurisdiction. Certainly Israel's neighbours were aware of the obligation of kings to provide for proper jurisdiction. In Babylon, Shamash the sun god was the special patron of justice. The inculcation of a proper concern in the field of justice was an aspect of the divine instruction that was continually emphasized. One of the prescriptions of the Ten Commandments concerns the proper evidence to be given in court. An ancient collection of laws in the book of the Covenant (Exod. 23.1–6, 6–9) provides a short examination of conscience for the judge. The Deuteronomic code provides precise regulations for the exercise of jurisdiction, including the right of appeal to the holy place (Deut. 16.18–20; 17.2–13); it insists twice on the necessity of providing at least two witnesses in the case of capital offences (Deut. 17.6; 19.15–21). The institution of jurisdiction is traced back to Moses in Exodus 18 and again in Deuteronomy 1.9–18. In Deuteronomy 1.17 there occurs the basic statement: 'Judgement belongs to God.' Because Israel loves Yahweh as the God of justice, it must accordingly love justice as it orders the relationships between men.

Justice in the Old Testament is never blind *Justitia*. It is always understood as an aspect of open-eyed compassion. It is then in the line of what has already been said when we insist in the second place that Israel from its very beginnings is aware of the divine demand for compassion towards the weak and the poor. This is clear from a very concrete instruction in the book of the Covenant: 'If you advance money to any poor man amongst my people, you shall not act like a money-lender.' A later hand has added: 'You must not exact interest in advance from him.' The original text continues: 'If you take your neighbour's cloak in pawn, you shall return it to him by sunset, because it is his only covering. It is the cloak in which he wraps his body; in what else can he sleep? If he appeals to me, I will listen, for I am full of compassion' (Exod. 22.24–6). Yahweh appears personally at the end of this sentence: 'I am full of compassion.' Because Israel loves this compassionate one, who has also been compassionate towards Israel, then must she be compassionate towards the neighbour.

In the subsequent addition to the text the taking of interest is forbidden without reservation. It can be confirmed that the prohibition of interest is emphatically maintained in every strand of the Old Testament (Lev. 25.36ff.; Deut. 23.20ff.; Ezek. 18.8, 13, 17 and 22.12; Ps. 15.5). Two remarks must be made to clarify this directive: first, Israel's surrounding world was thoroughly familiar with the practice of interest, and very high interest was exacted on a loan amounting even to a quarter or a third of what had been loaned.[6] Secondly, that epoch was not of course familiar with a loan made for the purposes of production; it had in mind only the consumer-type loan, i.e. it had regard only to the case of one who in economic straits pledged himself for food or money. The Old Testament is quite categoric in its demand that the need of the poor should not be the occasion for one's own enrichment.

On the other hand there are two further remarks to be made. The command does not presume the Diaspora situation, where the people live in the midst of strangers and for whom the land is to be set free. It lives still bordered by the land. The word *nokri*, which is used here, describes a stranger who is staying in the land for a short time; one would generally be thinking of a foreign businessman. For the 'alien who is at your door', as Deuteronomy says, i.e. the foreigner who is to live in the land for quite some time and who must look to protection from the inhabitants, the Old Testament uses the word *ger*, settler.[7] And it is significant that the alien, who becomes fully one's neighbour by actually settling, comes up again in a quite different series of commandments. The book of the Covenant (Exod. 22.21–4) has the following: 'You shall not wrong an alien, or be hard upon him.' A later hand has added the reason for this: 'You were yourselves aliens in Egypt. You shall not ill-treat any widow or fatherless child.' The text continues: 'If you do [i.e. oppress the alien] be sure that I will listen if they appeal to me.' And a yet later hand has enlarged this further: 'My anger will be aroused and I will kill you with the sword; your own wives shall become widows and your children fatherless.' It is clear from Deuteronomy 14.21 that the settler has not yet been taken up into the worshipping community of Israel. The injunction runs: 'You shall not eat anything that has died a natural death. You shall give it to the aliens who live in your settlements, and they may eat it, or you may sell it to a foreigner; for you are a people holy to the Lord your God.' From the cultic point of view the settler is equivalent to the foreign businessman to whom this flesh may be sold. It is quite impressive when Deuteronomy 24.17 insists: 'You shall not deprive aliens and orphans of justice nor take a widow's cloak in pledge.' The settler is placed on the same level as those persons who are specially in need of compassion. But Deuteronomy 10.19 goes far beyond this when, in the introductory address, we read: 'You too must love the alien, for you once lived as aliens in Egypt.' This same echoes even more loudly in Leviticus 19.33–4: 'When an alien settles with you in your land, you shall not oppress him. He shall be treated as a native born among you, and you shall love him as a man like yourself, because you were aliens in Egypt. I am the Lord your God.'

It is quite clear here that the stranger who has become a neighbour because of his long sojourn in Israel, is included fully in the demand for compassion. One is responsible for one's conduct towards him before God, who once liberated Israel.

Two further points are to be made in connection with this passage from Deuteronomy. It is to be noted that in the regulation dealing with the prohibition of interest, it speaks of one's 'brother'. 'You shall not take interest from your brother.' It is a specific development of what was said about mutual responsibility, that Deuteronomy does not speak in the current terminology of the neighbour, but of the brother among the people.[8] This terminology is used in the laws about the king (Deut. 17.14–20): 'You shall appoint over you a man of your own race' (v. 15); and there is the impressive admonition that the king 'shall not become prouder than his fellow-countrymen' (v. 20). Deuteronomy uses the same terminology when speaking of those of the people who have been sold into slavery: 'When a fellow-Hebrew, man or woman, sells himself to you as a slave he shall serve you for six years and in the seventh year you shall set him free' (15.12). The idea of brother in Deuteronomy embraces the people on every level of society. Israel is in this respect a stranger in its surrounding world where one will look in vain for the like.

The reason for this peculiar feature becomes clear as we read through the book of the Covenant up to the Law of Holiness: the people is always conscious of itself as a whole as it stands before the memory of Yahweh's liberating act at the Exodus from Egypt. This implies a striking relativization of the social differences which existed in Israel as well as in the neighbouring countries. In the presence of Yahweh whom Israel acknowledges as the Lord who liberated her, these differences become of a relative unimportance.

Because Deuteronomy shows a knowledge of what God's people is and a love of compassion in its God, it also reveals a sense of compassion for the weak in the formulation of its laws. Consequently it not only directs, as the book of the Covenant had already done, that the slave be freed in the seventh year; it prescribes further that the one who is freed should not be let go empty-handed. He must be given what is necessary in the matter of cattle, in the produce of the threshing floor and the wine press, so that he can establish himself once more in an independent way of life:

> But when you set him free, do not let him go empty-handed. Give to him lavishly from your flock, from your threshing-floor and your wine-press. . . . Remember that you were slaves in Egypt and the Lord your God redeemed you; that is why I am giving you this command today (Deut. 15.14).

When Deuteronomy is insisting on open-handedness towards a fellow-countryman and urging that he be loaned on pledge as much as he needs,[9] it goes on to insist:

> See that you do not harbour iniquitous thoughts when you find that the seventh year, the year of remission, is near, and look askance at your needy countryman and give him nothing. If you do, he will appeal to the Lord against you, and you will be found guilty of sin. Give freely to him and do not begrudge him your bounty, because it is for this very bounty that the Lord your God will bless you in everything that you do or undertake (Deut. 15.9–10).

The prescription of the book of the Covenant is that the cloak of a poor man which has been taken in pledge must be returned to him by nightfall; the Deuteronomic legislator, having regard for the more powerful creditor, adds the following protective clause: 'When you make a loan to another man, do not enter his house to take a pledge from him. Wait outside, and the man whose creditor you are shall bring the pledge out to you' (Deut. 24.10). In the context of this concern for human values there occurs the demand, quite unheard of in Babylonian law, that one must not surrender to his master a slave who has run away, but that he must be allowed to stay with the person to whom he had fled, anywhere he chooses (Deut. 23.16).

I would like to throw into relief the prescription that occurs first in the book of the Covenant (Exod. 23.4), and then in greater detail in Deuteronomy 22.1–4 to the effect that when a man sees an enemy's ox or ass lying helpless under his load, he must lend a hand with it; or when he meets an enemy's ox or ass straying, he shall take it back to him. Perhaps in this context one should also draw attention to the demand for compassion in respect of a bird brooding on its nest:

> When you come across a bird's nest by the road, in a tree or on the ground, with fledglings or eggs in it and the mother-bird on the nest, do not take both mother and young. Let the mother-bird go free, and take only the young; then you will prosper and live long.

All these gentle and quite humane qualities are found in Deuteronomy, which, when faced with the evil conduct which stains the people, demands with inexorable severity, no less than eight times: 'You must rid yourselves of this wickedness' (Deut. 13.6; 7.7, 12; 19.19; 21.21; 22.21–2, 24; 24.7). All this is demanded in respect of the God whom Israel must love, but who will tolerate no evil within his people.

In the Law of Holiness all these prescriptions stand under the demand to be holy, because Yahweh is holy. In the central chapter of Leviticus (19), over which this basic formula stands, as it were, as a headline, the most varied material is gathered together: there are special rubrics for cult beside basic directions for living which are found in part in the Decalogue; prescriptions for a healthy life, for a life governed by justice, for a life of pious respect for the weak and the old, for a life removed from all hidden evil. Quite objective, practical directions about leaving the remains of the harvest in the fields or in the vineyards, so that the poor and the settlers could make use of them, are found side by side with demands which would pluck evil by the roots from the very heart of man:

> You shall reprove your fellow-countryman frankly and so you will have no share in his guilt. You shall not seek revenge, or cherish anger towards your kinsfolk; you shall love your neighbour as a man like yourself. I am the Lord. (Lev. 19.17–18).

Such a life of holiness is to be lived out in the presence of Yahweh who presents himself personally and by name to the Israelites in his command. It is always a question of the holy one who has made Israel his holy people.

Israel meets this holy one in its worship. The commands of the Law of Holiness which, apart from Leviticus 19, close at times with the formula, 'I am Yahweh', or the fuller formula, 'I am Yahweh, your God',[10] allow one to sense in the background some liturgical proclamation of Yahweh. This background is quite recognizable in the great liturgical scene of the proclamation of the Decalogue in Exodus 20, where Yahweh introduces the ten basic principles of law with the self-revelation: 'I am the Lord your God who brought you out of Egypt, out of the land of slavery.' Psalms 50 and 81 stand as witnesses on either side of this scene and are a proof that the whole community of Israel was addressed liturgically in the proclamation of the Decalogue. It is quite proper then to see in the Old Testament prescriptions for worship how Israel, who even in her liturgical celebrations was not summoned out of her world, acknowledges beyond her world the Lord who wants to be remembered always as the Lord and giver of this world.

What was said about the law of Israel can be repeated about the liturgical life of Israel. The group of tribes who were indigenous to the land of Canaan have learnt much in their religious usage from the previous inhabitants of the land. This is especially clear from the older feast calendars of Israel.[11] All men must appear at the sanctuary three times a year, for the feast of the Mazzoth, the feast of the Harvest and the feast of Ingathering. Such are the prescriptions of the calendars of feasts in the book of the Covenant (Exod. 23.14–17), in the Yahwistic Decalogue (Exod. 34.14–26), and in Deuteronomy 16.1–17, with further developments. The unleavened bread, from which the first feast has its name, was a flat piece of bread made without yeast, i.e. there was abstention from the elements of the previous year's harvest. The Harvest feast began at the end of the harvesting of the corn, and the feast of the Ingathering in autumn at the conclusion of the vintage. In ancient times the great feast of the year took place at the conclusion of the economic year when one set about calculating for the new year. It was only the Assyrian domination towards the end of the eighth century that gave Palestine the calendar of Mesopotamia with spring as the beginning of the year.[12]

The three great festivals were originally directed to the cycle of the agricultural year and the harvest of the field and the vineyard. It is quite interesting, then, to see how Yahweh enters into this purely agricultural character as the proper lord of these feasts. In the case of the feast of the Mazzoth, there was an old nomad custom of slaughtering a lamb (the Pasch)[13] which occurred at about the same time of the year; at a very early stage it was associated with the exodus from Egypt; it began to dominate the custom and real significance of eating unleavened bread, and to give it a completely new direction. As a consequence the unleavened bread was understood as a sign which recalled the hasty exodus from Egypt when there was not enough time to leaven the dough.[14] Together with the paschal custom of smearing the doorposts and the lintel with blood, which was meant to keep alive the memory of the slaying of the first-born of the Egyptians and the sparing of the Israelites, the feast of Pasch-Mazzoth became the great feast of the praise of God who had led Israel out of the slavery of Egypt.

In the case of the great autumn feast, which was later known as the feast of tents, the course of events is not so clear. According to Leviticus 23.39–43 Israel had to live in tents, made out of branches, for seven days, to remind the people of the period of wandering in the desert when they did not yet live in houses, 'so that your descendants may be reminded how I made the Israelites live in tents when I brought them out of Egypt'. When the Jewish community hung up the seven fruits of the promised land in the tents made out of branches, it emphasized even more the goal of the wandering in the desert, namely life in the land and enjoyment of its produce. The least significant of the three feasts took longest to receive its new orientation, and is celebrated in the Christian community as the feast of Pentecost. In the period after Old Testament times this feast occurs as the commemoration of the giving of the law to Moses on the mountain. Here too it is the God who led Israel out of Egypt to his mountain on Sinai to make his will known to her, who is the centre of the celebration.

Besides this process which took over and gradually gave a new stamp to certain pious customs, there was at work the opposite process, that of decisive and total rejection of practices which could not be assimilated. It was precisely because Israel was concerned with the holy one, who permitted no other side-by-side with him, that there was this sharper rejection of the institution of ritual prostitution at Israel's holy places (Deut. 23.18ff.). There were certain mourning customs, which seem originally to have been concerned with self-mutilation in the presence of one appearing from the dead. Israel realized that commerce with these powers was forbidden. They were incompatible with the holiness of Yahweh to whom alone Israel was bound:

> You are the sons of the Lord your God: you shall not gash yourselves nor shave your forelocks in mourning for the dead. You are a people holy to the Lord your God, and the Lord has chosen you out of all peoples on earth to be his special possession (Deut. 14.1–2).

In Leviticus 19.27ff. this command appears with the closing formula: 'I am the Lord.' From the very beginning it is clear that the law of Israel could give no place to the cultic symbol of Ashera (the sacred pole), which would preserve in its name the memory of the Canaanite goddess (Deut. 16.21). Later, the symbol of the memorial stone, the Mazzebah, which had been quite harmless in ancient times,[15] was sharply rejected (Deut. 16.22; Lev. 26.1). This was due to the connection of such stones with the worship of Baal on the high places. Israelite law rejected with increasing vigour every sort of sorcery, divination, soothsaying, which was widespread in the world of that time. The 'prophetic code' of Deuteronomy 18.9–22 contrasts all this with that prophecy which alone was legitimate in Israel and which was seen as a continuation of the office of Moses. It is not a process of spiritualization which would withdraw Israel from the concrete problems of the world; rather it is a question of a summons of its unique Lord to the rites and piety of his world.[16]

Yahweh, zealous for his unique position, prevailed in the worship of Israel. In the course of history this occurred in such a way in respect to the place in which God was honoured, as to distinguish the people of Yahweh ever more clearly from the public

worship of her neighbours. In the Deuteronomic reform at the end
of the seventh century, whose spiritual background is the collection of Yahweh's commands in the book of Deuteronomy, King
Josiah did away with all the sacred places of worship in the land,
even those supported by the venerable tradition of the patriarchs,
and proclaimed Jerusalem as the only legitimate place in his realm
where Yahweh could be worshipped. 'Hear, O Israel, the Lord is
our God, one Lord.' This introductory sentence of the *Shema* is
the *leit-motiv* of the measures which are further developed and
detailed in Deuteronomy 12. Whatever one may think about
secondary influences, cultic or religio-political, one must not
overlook in these demands of Deuteronomy and in their execution
by the king, a definitive attitude towards Yahweh with all that
this implies, which marks him off from the gods of the surrounding world. One God and one place of worship, which this holy,
free Lord of Israel has chosen for himself; this is the way in which
Israel is to worship her God.

The assent to these demands of Deuteronomy is not given in
any spirit of gloomy, iconoclastic legalism. The background is
rather the great joy which Yahweh has in choosing this place
where his name is to dwell in the midst of his people and in in-
viting them to be near him:

> Then you shall bring everything that I command you to the place
> which the Lord your God will choose as a dwelling for his
> Name—your whole-offerings and sacrifices, your tithes and con-
> tributions, and all the choice gifts that you have vowed to the Lord.
> You shall rejoice before the Lord your God with your sons and
> daughters, your male and female slaves, and the Levites who live in
> your settlements because they have no holding or patrimony among
> you (Deut. 12.11–12).

The place of nearness to Yahweh is a place where all, right down
to children, slaves, and the Levites who have no patrimony,
should be happy in his presence.

One may ask about the motive for bringing these offerings to
the holy place. Besides the readiness to say thanks with a gift,
as is so beautifully expressed in the prayer of the peasant in
Deuteronomy 26, there was in ancient Israel the idea of the community meal in God's presence at the holy place.

It is important here to add something which is essential to one's whole view of the Old Testament. The writings of the pre-exilic prophets, for example Amos 5.21ff., or even of Jeremiah, contain passionate attacks against cultic celebration and against sacrifice. Jeremiah 7.1ff. even attacks the confidence in nearness to God in the holy place and the sense of security in being there. The terrible possibility is here considered that zeal for the worship of God can suppress what is foremost in God's will, concrete responsibility for one's neighbour and the poor. As the people flocked to the temple and in doing so forgot the simple demands of proper social relationships, Jeremiah threatened that the temple would be judged and become a heap of ruins just like the ancient temple in Shiloh, which had been destroyed in the wars with the Philistines (Jer. 7.13ff.; 26.6). This threat of judgement soon became a grim reality.

After the disaster of the Babylonian exile, Israel consolidated herself within the Persian empire as a sort of church-state organization in and round Jerusalem. Ever conscious of this disaster, Israel became aware in a quite different way that she could only live if her guilt was continually being removed. This is reflected in the instructions for sacrifice; the sacrifice for sin,[17] whose roots and ritual would go back to a more ancient period, takes on an ever greater significance. It should be noted that in the great calendar of sacrifices of Numbers 28ff., a sacrifice for sin has been added to the other sacrifices in each of the three great feasts of the year. The pattern is to be found in the exilic instructions for festal sacrifice in Ezekiel 45.18–25. Nothing like this is to be found in the calendar of Deuteronomy 16 which is characterized by the joyful note of thanksgiving.

In the period after the great disaster, attention is concentrated on the feast which gradually became the most impressive of all, the great day of Atonement, which was celebrated with a strict fast (Lev. 23.26–32). Leviticus 16 describes the ritual of the purification of the holy place which developed into a community feast: in the solemn act of atonement, the high priest is empowered to lay his hands on the head of a goat, so transferring to it all the sins of Israel, and to drive it out into the wilderness to where it carries upon itself all the iniquities of the people. Israel thereby expresses how deeply conscious she is of being reliant upon the forgiving compassion of God. 'This shall become a rule binding on you for all time, to make for the Israelites once a year the expiation required by all their sins' (v. 34). We stand once more where we stood at the end of the previous chapter. Israel, who has survived the great catastrophes of judgement, knows that she has life and future only through the grace and favour of her God; every year she must remove her guilt in a solemn liturgical act which he has prescribed.

But what do life and future mean? What has the Old Testament to say of life and death? This will be the subject of the next chapter.

9

DEATH AND LIFE

At the international congress for the study of the Old Testament which was held in Göttingen in 1935, H. Wheeler Robinson, the Oxford Old Testament scholar, gave a lecture entitled 'The Hebrew Conception of Corporate Personality'.[1] It has had a very notable effect. He showed how in Old Testament thought not only the individual person, but also a whole community can be treated as a personality, as a corporate personality. And this personality includes not only those who are alive at the moment, but also the ancestors and the posterity. It is not to be regarded merely as a literary personification or as an ideal figure, but quite realistically as a living entity. And so in speaking, one can move without more ado from the individual member to the collective entity and back; and it is not correct to set the individual in fundamental opposition to the collectivity.

Wheeler Robinson has certainly focused attention on a genuine aspect of Old Testament thinking. Israel sees her early history present in the individual figures of the patriarchs, so that each individual Israelite can withdraw within the ever-present corporate personality. On the other hand the Israelite farmer, whose thanksgiving prayer for the harvest we have mentioned earlier,[2] narrates in his prayer the whole story of his people in the Exodus and the taking of the land; he has taken part personally in this history: '... the Lord brought us out of Egypt ... brought us to this place and gave us this land ... and now I have brought the firstfruits of the soil which thou, O Lord, hast given me' (Deut. 26.8ff.). Both these attitudes show the constant to and fro movement in the presentation of Israel's history, which can be portrayed as the story of an all-embracing corporate personality, as well as of the individual member of the people.

The great images in which Israel is called out of Egypt as a son (Hos. 11.1), or presented as the spouse of Yahweh (Hos. 2.4ff.; Jer. 2.2; Ezek. 16.23), are more than mere poetic descriptions. They include a reality. In Hosea's image of the son who was called out of Egypt, and Ezekiel's description of the two women whose youth was spent in Egypt, as well as in Jeremiah's description of the happy marriage in the desert period, concrete historical memories are woven quite ingenuously into the narrative of Israel as a corporate personality in the form of son, wife, or the two women.

In Ezekiel 16 the prophet has thrown light on the very beginning of Jerusalem's history, in which the history of Israel is played out poetically, with the image of the woman whom Yahweh has taken as his wife. We have spoken of this passage in an earlier context[3] (see chapter 7). Yahweh found Jerusalem as a foundling destined to die. Her purely natural beginnings would mark Israel out as a being destined to death. 'Then I came by and saw you kicking helplessly in your own blood; I spoke to you, there in your blood, and bade you live.' Jerusalem, Israel owes its whole existence to Yahweh and his decision: 'Live!'

Israel continues to live in this knowledge. 'Life' is for Israel, as we have seen in an earlier context, precisely 'life in the land'. Israel must always remember that she is not native to the land, but that she has received it as a gift from Yahweh. She knows then from the very beginning that her 'life' comes from the hand of Yahweh. The period of political danger can only heighten this conviction. The history of the patriarchs makes it clear that Israel cannot take for granted her existence as a people. Genesis tells feelingly of the long wait for the childless ancestors. After Abraham, Isaac too had to entreat the Lord earnestly in prayer on behalf of his wife Rebecca who was without children. Throughout all this it was Yahweh's fidelity to his promise to Abraham, and this alone, that ensured the existence of the people as a people.

Israel knows that this promise is her support and her guarantee of life. In the light of this solemn promise it is quite astonishing that the problem of the life and death of the individual is not a pressing question in the Old Testament.

The Yahwistic account of the primeval events certainly touches the problem; it tells of the curse imposed upon man, who as one created from the dust must return to the dust, and who is driven out of the garden and must remain separated from the tree of life. The story of the blessing given to Abraham in Genesis 12.1–3 is a counterbalance to this story of the curse. This blessing, with its promise of a future and a people, is, according to the Yahwist, the complete counterbalance to the gloomy pronouncement of the primeval curse. When, then, the future and with it the life of Israel had been assured in Abraham's son, it can be said of him, without any further question being raised: 'He died at a good old age, after a very long life, and was gathered to his father's kin' (Gen. 25.8). The same is said of Isaac in Genesis 35.29 and, in a shortened form, of Jacob in 49.33.

Deuteronomy 34 reports the death of Moses. The death of the man who had brought the people out of Egypt to Mount Sinai and then to the very frontiers of the promised land, does not raise any particular question. A slightly bitter note attends his death from Deuteronomy 3.23ff., inasmuch as Yahweh does not allow him to enter the promised land. Everything that he had done had been directed to this; but because of the sinfulness of the people whose guilt he bears, Moses cannot enter. But Israel, who may cross over into the land, remains still under the promise of Yahweh.

Certain expressions from the Psalms and indirectly, too, some prophetic oracles make it quite clear that the express promise of life to the community and thereby to the individual as well took place at the holy shrines. Here, where it was believed Yahweh was present, were the sources of life.[4] Psalm 36, which beyond its mere material object hides a much deeper spiritual meaning, makes express use of this image when it describes the blessedness of staying near to Yahweh:

> How precious is thy steadfast love, O God!
> The children of men take refuge in the shadow of thy wings.
> They feast on the abundance of thy house,
> and thou givest them a drink from the river of thy delights.
> For with thee is the fountain of life;
> in thy light do we see light (vv. 7–9, RSV).

In other places we hear how the pilgrims long for the sanctuary, so as to meet there the living God. It is he who is the source of life. Psalm 42.1ff. speaks as follows of this longing for the sanctuary from afar:

> As a hind longs for the running streams,
> so do I long for thee, O God.
> With my whole being I thirst for God, the living God.
> When shall I come to God and appear in his presence?

Psalm 84 begins with the cry of joy of the pilgrim who is at the holy place:

> How dear is thy dwelling-place,
> thou Lord of Hosts!
> I pine, I faint with longing
> for the courts of the Lord's temple;
> my whole being cries out with joy
> to the living God.

In a discussion of the priestly Torah, J. Begrich has demonstrated that in certain places the prophet Amos clearly imitates the style of the priestly instruction at the sanctuary, but reverses completely its content.[5] We read in 5.4:

> These are the words of the Lord to the people of Israel:
> Resort to me, if you would live, not to Bethel;
> go not to Gilgal, nor pass on to Beersheba. . . .

One can recognize behind this the priestly instruction which runs: 'Resort to Bethel if you would live.' Look for sanctuary, there you will receive the promise of life.

Before going further into the question which immediately presents itself, namely what does this promise of life really mean for the individual, we must present with all clarity that peculiar quality which makes Old Testament faith something quite special in the religious history of its surrounding world—the unique way in which the Old Testament, apart from a few marginal remarks, never oversteps the threshold of the 'this side' in its expectations. This peculiar quality which makes of the Old Testament a book which is predominantly 'worldly' and bound to the 'this side', is always noted with a certain embarrassment. One has seen here one of the limits of the Old Testament which makes it, in comparison with the New Testament, a book of lesser rank.[6] God, freedom, and immortality are since Kant the unconditional religious postulates of the moral reason. The Old Testament, which says nothing of immortality, has appeared then to that type of Christianity which is coloured by idealism to be a book clearly less than Christian in a worldliness which is bound to this side of the grave.

The Old Testament certainly has something to say about death and what happens to man in death.[7] We can think of the narrative of Genesis 23, which we have already mentioned,[8] in which the main point at issue was that Abraham could legally acquire a piece of land in the promised land where he could bury Sarah. We have also cited the formula from Genesis 25.8 in which the same priestly tradition says that Abraham was gathered to his father's kin. The rest of the family lies at rest in the family grave. Speaking of the kings of Udah, the book of Kings continually repeats that a king 'rested with his forefathers and was buried with them in the city of David' (1 Kings 14.31; 15.24, etc.). It is clearly a part of the proper entry into the rest of death that a man is buried in the place where his forefathers were buried. An improper burial had something horrible about it, as the Old Testament parallel to the Greek story of Antigone in 2 Samuel 21 shows. In none of these places is anything more said than that the person was laid to rest; nothing is said about the state of the dead when laid with his forefathers.

The Old Testament speaks of Sheol, the realm of the underworld, Hades, into which the dead enter as shades. It is a quite unbalanced picture and has no clear connection with what is said of burial. Israel shares in the presentations of the underworld such as appear in the Babylonian netherworld, on the twelve tablets of the Gilgamesh epic,[9] and also in the netherworld of the *Odyssey*. Jacob, for example, who according to the priestly writer is buried later in the grave of his fathers, can say: 'You will bring down my grey hairs in sorrow to the grave' (Gen. 42.38; 44.29, 31). Most impressive of all in this respect are some of the prophetic oracles against the nations which describe the journey into Hades of certain enemy kings and powers. Isaiah 14.4ff. describes satirically the fall into the depths of Sheol of a great Mesopotamian ruler who wanted to make himself like the morning star and sit enthroned on the mountain of the gods. One element of the description is worthy of note. In Sheol are all the other great kings who have died before him. They receive the new arrival with the words: 'So you too are weak as we are, and have become one of us!' And mockingly they ask:

> Is this, they will say, the man who shook the earth,
> who made kingdoms quake,

> who turned the world into a desert
> and laid its cities in ruins,
> who never let his prisoners go free to their homes . . .?[10]

In contrast to the kings who 'lie all of them in honour, each in his last home', this king has 'been flung out unburied, mere loathsome carrion'. Shortly before, it is said of him who has been thrown down from his lofty place:

> Your pride and all the music of your lutes
> have been brought down to Sheol;
> maggots are the pallet beneath you,
> and worms your coverlet.[11]

The motif is found also in the oracles against the nations in the book of Ezekiel with further developments (26.20; 31.13, 15.18). The most impressive development occurs in Ezekiel 32.17ff., where together with the description of the grave and Sheol, the graves of the great powers, Assur, Elam, and Meshech-Tubal, together with all their troops, are mentioned. The honourable burial of the heroes of the past is so different from this disgraceful burial: 'They have gone down to Sheol with their weapons, their swords under their heads and their shields over their bones.'[12] Such descriptions, with their gloomy and gruesome background of the world of the dead, are at work in the Old Testament. What is significant for the Old Testament is that the underworld is not in the remotest way linked with Yahweh, the living God. It is utterly unthinkable for basic Old Testament belief that there should be a second god who was the lord below. There is not the slightest indication in any of these places of the idea of a lord of the underworld, who was familiar to the world of Israel. These aspects of the world picture remain quite untouched by the faith of Israel, and free from any theological implications; they are purely descriptive. The Old Testament gives the most severe admonitions against the use of occult means to enter into any form of relationship with this world and thereby to conjure powers from it. The collections of laws in the Old Testament indicate that there were always attempts to do this. There are vehement prohibitions against it (Lev. 19.31 and 20.6, 27; Deut. 18.11). Under Josiah all those who called up ghosts and spirits together with all other purveyors of necromancy and of strange gods were driven out of the land (2 Kings 23.24). The report is preserved in

1 Samuel 28.3 that Saul purged the land of all who trafficked with ghosts and spirits.

Something must be said in this context about that chapter of the history of Saul (1 Sam. 28) which seems to stand like an erratic block in the Old Testament. It is told how Saul, who himself had banished purveyors of necromancy from the land, consulted a woman who practised necromancy. He was in dire straits in face of the Philistine threat, he had consulted the Lord, but the Lord had not answered; he went therefore to the 'witch' of Endor and prevailed on her to conjure up the spirit of Samuel. It took place in the dead of night, and the woman did not know that it was Saul who had demanded of her to call up Samuel. It seems that it was the woman alone who was able to see the ghost; she described him to Saul, who then carried on the conversation with him. To Samuel's indignant question: 'Why have you disturbed me and brought me up?', Saul complains that he is at an utter loss in face of the Philistines and that God has remained completely silent. Samuel asks further: 'Why do you ask me, now that God has turned from you and become your adversary? He has done what he foretold through me.' He then recalls Saul's disobedience during the campaign against the Amalekites, which was the cause of the rejection of his kingship (1 Sam. 15). And he concludes what he has to say with the concrete prophecy: ' . . . tomorrow you and your sons shall be with me. Yes, indeed, the Lord will give the Israelite army into the hands of the Philistines.' Saul collapsed on the ground, terrified by Samuel's words, and it was only with difficulty that the woman and those who accompanied Saul were able to force him to eat a little and so regain something of his strength. On the following day the king and his sons fell in the battle against the Philistines.

This narrative combines in a unique way the worldly conception of the underworld with a sharp rejection of any commerce with it. This world exists in the imagery of Old Testament belief. The dead who have been laid in their graves are at rest there, though the Old Testament has nothing to say about them. Here one is disturbed from his rest and brought to speak with one of the living. The one who is alive wants to obtain secret information and to exercise power over an area where the living do not have power; what does he hear? It is only with difficulty that one can refrain from describing it as a deep psychological experience, and coming to the conclusion that it is Saul's uneasy conscience that speaks. Samuel in death does not tell Saul anything which he had not told him when he was alive. What is at most new is the sinister actualization of the message which the living Samuel had already pronounced about Saul: 'Tomorrow you and your sons shall be with me.' The destruction of Saul is imminent. In any case it is clear that this shadowy figure who returns from the dead has nothing different or more to say than what Yahweh had communicated through him when he was alive. No other voice is heard from the world of the dead than the voice of the Lord, the voice which Israel had already heard in the ordinary course of its life.

This isolated and marginal story only confirms in its own way what was stated at the beginning: Israel and the individual in Israel hear the voice of Yahweh in their daily life and in the things that concern it. Whatever Israel's neighbours may have believed about a further life and further activity after death, as well as of the godly powers in this area beyond, has withered in Israel itself.

This is astonishing, especially when we realize the great importance of belief in some sort of continuation of life beyond the grave in the surrounding world. The cycle of nature must surely have suggested such reflection in those religions which reverenced the gods as the embodiments of the powers of nature. The grain is buried in the earth; after the long winter does it not mysteriously come alive again and of its own dynamism shoot forth new life? We know something of the phenomenon of what are called grain mummies from ancient Egypt. Grains of corn are scattered around a mummy on a stretcher, watered and awakened to new life.[13] Egypt reverences Osiris in the form of a god who embodies in his life-cycle such dying and coming to life again.[14] Such customs as the lament for Osiris, the lament with his grieving companion, the goddess Isis, the search for the corpse of the righteous Osiris killed by the evil Seth, were cult forms deeply engrained in the hearts and sentiments of the pious.

Mesopotamia had a similar belief about the god Tammuz. Ezekiel reports (8.14) that he was taken back in a vision to the gateway of the temple of Jerusalem. He saw women who sat there wailing for Tammuz: an indication of how in times of religious corruption such practices crept in even to the temple of Jerusalem.[15] So too the 'sacred oaks' and 'garden shrines'[16] which delighted the people in Isaiah 1.29,[17] and the 'gardens in honour of Adonis' and 'your cuttings for a foreign god' (Isa. 17.10), are symbols of this nature religion which aims at calling attention to the ever-awakening life of the plants that are preserved there. The 'pleasant plants' and the 'alien god' call up the Phoenician god Adonis; the Greek world had already carried stories of his early death and the lament over it.[18] The opinion that in Hosea 6.1ff. the text of an ancient hymn to Adonis may well have been preserved in a proverb-like form, is not to be rejected out of hand. The hymn of repentance runs:

> Come, let us return to the Lord;
> for he has torn us and will heal us.
> . . .
> after two days he will revive us,
> on the third day he will restore us,
> that in his presence we may live.

The phrases could well have been shaped by the story of the resurrection of Adonis of whom Lucian relates (*De Dea Syria,* 6)[19] that he came to life again on the day after the offering for the dead was laid before him.

There is no place at all for this in the Yahweh faith, be it in the commandments, the prophets, or the Psalms. Yahweh is the living God and as such the god of the living, whom he deals with in life this side of the grave and to whom he dispenses life from the sanctuary.

We are faced here yet again with the question: what is meant by the word 'life'?

The answer to this question is clearest in the Psalms, especially in the Psalms of lament, which cry out to Yahweh for help, and in the Psalms of thanksgiving, which praise Yahweh for the help which has been experienced. And the answer becomes even clearer when the question asks, not primarily about life, but rather about death. In his dissertation 'Deliverance from Death in the Individual Laments and Thanksgiving Hymns of the Old Testament', C. Barth has said something extremely important.[20] He has demonstrated that 'death' in the Psalms does not mean simply the physical death of the person who is praying, but indicates on a much broader scale a threat to man. According to Barth's formulation, death is a 'realm'. It is a world of opposition which threatens the living and which aims at preventing man from dying 'old and full of days', i.e. after a life lived out to fullness until his natural powers fade. Death robs man of the normal length of time which God has assigned him. Heralds which threaten such death are hunger, weakness, and illness. Part of such weakening is the experience of insult and infamy, poverty and deprivation. In all these phenomena which can threaten man, the sinister powers of the world of the dead, which is a world of darkness, force their way into the life of man. It is taken quite for granted by Old Testament faith that these powers can have no power at all over man if Yahweh wards them off. Behind these powers there cannot be a second power in opposition to Yahweh. The believer therefore turns to Yahweh amid all these incursions of Sheol, the world of death, which try to overpower him, and cries to him to frighten them away. And when he is finally delivered from these threats, he thanks Yahweh as his saviour for delivering him and guaranteeing him life.

Psalm 18 describes quite dramatically this event in which God dispenses life: it is the picture of a divine intervention from heaven which reaches into the depths of Sheol, which had already stretched out its claws to drag down the Psalmist:

> When the bonds of death held me fast,
> destructive torrents overtook me,
> the bonds of Sheol tightened round me,
> the snares of death were set to catch me;
> then in anguish of heart I cried to the Lord,
> I called for help to my God;
> he heard me from his temple,
> and my cry reached his ears.
> The earth heaved and quaked,
> the foundations of the mountains shook;
> they heaved, because he was angry.
> Smoke rose from his nostrils,
> devouring fire came out of his mouth,
> glowing coals and searing heat.
> He swept the skies aside as he ascended,
> thick darkness lay under his feet.
> He rode on a cherub, he flew through the air;
> he swooped on the wings of the wind.
> . . .

He reached down from the height and took me,
he drew me out of mighty waters,
he rescued me from my enemies, strong as they were,
from my foes when they grew too powerful for me.
They confronted me in the hour of my peril,
but the Lord was my buttress.
He brought me out into an open place,
he rescued me because he delighted in me.

The hymns of lament and thanksgiving are often a cause of embarrassment for one who seeks to understand them. What, in the
individual case, is the concrete distress by which the Psalmist is
threatened? Is it a particular sickness, is it false friends, or is it
some material threat? The threat is never the simple possibility of
death through old age. Even in Psalm 71, the only clear example of
the prayer of an old man who prays in verse 9, 'Do not cast me off
when old age comes, nor forsake me when my strength fails', there
is no petition for survival beyond death.

Quite concrete threats can surround the Psalmist at times. This
is clear from Psalm 107, which sets side by side the individual circumstances of those coming to the sanctuary with their gifts.
Those who have returned from a dangerous journey are called
upon to give thanks, they have been 'redeemed by him from the
power of the enemy and gathered out of every land . . .'

Some lost their way in desert wastes;
they found no road to a city to live in;
hungry and thirsty,
their spirit sank within them.
So they cried to the Lord in their trouble,
and he rescued them from their distress;
he led them by a straight and easy way
until they came to a city to live in.

Then there are those who have been freed from prison:

Some sat in darkness, dark as death,
prisoners bound fast in iron,
because they had rebelled against God's commands
and flouted the purpose of the Most High.
Their spirit was subdued by hard labour;
they stumbled and fell with none to help them.
So they cried to the Lord in their trouble,

> and he saved them from their distress;
> he brought them out of darkness, dark as death,
> and broke their chains.

Those who have been delivered from illness are called upon:

> Some were fools,[21] they took to rebellious ways,
> and for their transgression they suffered punishment.
> They sickened at the sight of food
> and drew near to the very gates of death.
> So they cried to the Lord in their trouble,
> and he saved them from their distress;
> he sent his word to heal them
> and bring them alive out of the pit of death.

Finally a fourth group is called upon, those 'who go to sea in ships'. They had experienced a severe storm at sea, they had cried out to Yahweh, and he had saved them:

> Let them thank the Lord for his enduring love
> and for the marvellous things he has done for men.
> Let them exalt him in the assembly of the people
> and praise him in the council of the elders.

Such precise descriptions of concrete troubles, out of which men cried to God, are rather rare. As a rule there is a general description which covers afflictions of the most different kind. As an example reference could be made to Psalm 22, the Psalm which Christ recited during his Passion. The deepseated longing of all these Psalms of petition comes to full expression in this accumulation of distress. In all these troubles, the appeal is always that Yahweh would turn his gracious countenance to the Psalmist. It is in this that life consists. 'Make thy face shine upon us that we may be saved' is the refrain of the lament in Psalm 80. The individual member of the community experiences life in Yahweh's renewed attention.

This promise of life takes place in a special way in the sanctuary where the community is gathered together—as has already been pointed out. It has perhaps been noticed that the same prayer is made in the refrain of Psalm 80 as in the blessing of Numbers 6.24–6; here Aaron, the high priest, is told to pronounce over the assembled community:

The Lord bless you and watch over you;
The Lord make his face shine upon you
and be gracious to you;
the Lord look kindly on you and give you peace.

All these blessings and phrases describe basically what is meant by 'life': protection, grace, favour from the brightness of Yahweh's face which is turned towards them, all of which banishes the darkness of death.

However, one must not approach this area of life without preparation. As we have already seen in detail, Yahweh, in his dealings with his people, is always the holy one who demands obedience. Attention has long since been drawn to the formula which would have had its setting in life in the approach to the gate of the temple[22] (Ps. 15 and 24.3–6; Isa. 33.14b–16). One speaks of the Gate Liturgy or, because it is an instruction as to how one is to comport oneself before God, the Torah Liturgy.

The situation is described at the beginning of Psalm 15:

O Lord, who may lodge in thy tabernacle?
Who may dwell on thy holy mountain?

The pilgrim is standing at the gate of the temple and asking the condition for admittance. There follows the answer given to him by a priest guarding the entrance:

The man of blameless life, who does what is right
and speaks the truth from his heart;
who has no malice on his tongue,
who never wrongs a friend
and tells no tales against his neighbour;
. . .
who does not put his money out to usury
and takes no bribe against an innocent man.

The conclusion, which in the set formula pronounced admission, is changed to a general oracle of salvation: 'He who does these things shall never be brought low.' The conclusion of the corresponding section in Psalm 24.5 is even clearer: 'He shall receive a blessing from the Lord, and justice from God his saviour.' The whole is concerned with admission to the place where the blessing is promised and with it help is dispensed. Blessing is in parallelism to 'righteousness', which God gives the one who is permitted to enter the sanctuary. The idea of the help that will be granted to the pilgrim is certainly to the fore. But the word has a far wider resonance than this.

This can be clarified from Ezekiel 18, a text spoken by the prophet to one oppressed but in a quite different situation.[23] The prophet seems to be making use of elements of the Gate Liturgy in a modified form. The pilgrim's entrance question is no longer heard; there is, however, a succession of divine demands which are used to describe one who is obedient to Yahweh. This is followed by what seems to be the concluding pronouncement of the priest, preserved in a more complete and more original form:

> Consider the man who is righteous and does what is just and right. He never feasts at mountain-shrines, never lifts his eyes to the idols of Israel. . . . He oppresses no man, he returns the debtor's pledge, he never robs. He gives bread to the hungry and clothes to those who have none. He never lends either at a discount or at interest. He shuns injustice and deals fairly between man and man . . . . Such a man is righteous; he shall live, says the Lord God (Ezek. 18.5–9).

These demands on the members of the people of Yahweh contain much that is known to us from what has been said in an earlier context. It is a question here of what is contained in the two parts of the closing formula: 'Such a man is righteous: he shall live, says the Lord God.' The first part contains an element which in form is quite characteristic of a priestly decision; it has been described as a declaratory judgement.[24] The priest declares over the pilgrim, who confirms that he has observed all that has been demanded of him: 'He is righteous.' It is a word of praise and is not to be understood as an automatic approval of the observance of a list of virtues. It is a judgement of Yahweh: this man is righteous in my eyes, he may enter my sanctuary: 'He may lodge in my tabernacle, dwell on my holy mountain', as Psalm 15 says. But something else is immediately bound up with this: 'He shall live.' And so it is confirmed that entrance to the sanctuary means entrance to the promise of life. 'For with thee is the fountain of life', as Psalm 36.9 has said.

This background gives access to much in the Psalms and to many of their strange worldly qualities. What is the source of that extraordinary daring of so many Psalms where the Psalmist expresses his own guiltlessness? This is not smug self-righteousness; it is an echo of the divine decision, 'he is righteous'. Many Psalms make it clear that the Psalmist is fully conscious of his righteousness which has been given him as a gift in the forgiveness of sins.[25]

It opens the way to an understanding of the vehemence, often so strange to us, with which the Psalmist, within the context of the world, campaigns against his enemies, as well as against all those things which sound attack, and in which he sees the world of the dead rising against him. It is a complete misunderstanding to interpret these Psalms as merely the angry outbursts of a vengeful disposition. The question is always before the Psalmist: does the approval of his righteousness come from God? Is the assurance of life valid? Behind all this, whatever human element may here and there have become embedded, there is ultimately the struggle with God, the bestower of grace, who has pledged himself to man in the midst of his trial through illness, distress, and enemy.

The Old Testament faith must struggle through all this, taking 'the world' this side of the grave with complete earnestness, without the cheap option of a withdrawal into a dream world beyond, and without the supports which the world picture of the surrounding religions offered with their belief in a resurrection from the dead.

The very pressing question now arises, whether such a worldly Old Testament has not something to say about a hope for the future, for Israel and for the individual believer, and beyond Israel of a hope for the world.

10

THE HOPE OF ISRAEL
AND THE HOPE OF
THE WORLD

The exposition of the very marked this-worldliness of the Old Testament concluded with the question of the hope of Old Testament belief. The point of departure for the discussion of this question may seem very remote.

Israel understood her call from the slavery of Egypt as a call to life. Israel experienced historical confirmation of this call in the gift of the land, in defence against her enemies in the period of the Judges, and finally in the mission of David as the definitive liberator from Philistine oppression (1 Sam. 9.16). The older accounts in the Old Testament do not show any serious reflection on the possibility of a broader future. They show pleasure in what life offers at the moment, and in the liberation, and they praise Yahweh for this. This is the case in the song of Deborah, as well as in the ancient narratives of the Judges, and also in the accounts of the rise of the monarchy.

It is during the reign of David that there first comes from the lips of a prophet an oracle of promise for the future. Whatever judgement one may make about the original historical circumstance of Nathan's promise to the house of David,[1] there is no mistaking that in Judah, the rather limited area over which the house of David ruled, it made history and determined the life of the state for a period of 400 years. This prophecy promised to David that Yahweh would make David's son his own son and that the royal house of David would last for ever.

There can be no doubt that, as a result of more recent research, the promise about the dynasty as well as the promise that the king is to be the son of God, cannot be understood outside the context of the royal ideology of Israel's surrounding world.[2] Such ideas had taken root in the Canaanite city of Jerusalem long before the time of David; and they had to take a different form when resumed by a prophet of Yahweh, the God of Israel, who had prepared a people for himself and had promised it life. They had to share in that extraordinary involvement of the whole nation which was characteristic of this faith. Yahweh could not be the God of the dynasty in the narrow sense; if he were, the dynasty would not be so significant historically. He remains God of his people over whom he is Lord and through whom he wants to base his dominion on earth. The dynasty remains attorney in the area in which Yahweh's dominion is the really decisive factor.

This is clear too in the Psalms, where the general lines of the royal ideology are clearly delineated, for example, Psalms 2 and 110, hymns of the enthronement of the king of Jerusalem. Psalm 110 consists basically of two divine oracles which are addressed to the king on the day of his enthronement. One addresses the king in the form of an oath made by Yahweh: 'You are a priest for ever, in the succession of Melchizedek.' When the following verse speaks of the dominion of this king over his enemies, and says 'the Lord is at your right hand', one would see this dominion as the central point of the oracle. But when he is invited to sit at the right hand of Yahweh, then it is being proclaimed that Yahweh is the real king. He takes the Davidic king to be his co-regent. This royal lordship of Yahweh comes fully to the fore in Psalm 2. The first strophe describes the rebellion of the subject nations, which was a common event in the great empires with the coming of a new king. A second strophe describes how from his throne in heaven Yahweh laughs to scorn this revolt, but then in his anger reminds the nations of his protective hand over the king of Zion: 'I have enthroned my king on Zion my holy mountain.' There follows in a third strophe the quite unique passage where Yahweh makes a promise to his king which has been compared with the royal protocol of Egypt.[3] The king is described as the son of God: 'You are my son, this day I become your father.' The linking of 'this day' with the phrase 'become' (literally, 'this day I have begotten you') makes it clear that it is a question of a figure of speech for the adoption of the king as son. The king is then allowed to make a wish: 'Ask of me what you will.' The account of the dream of Solomon at Gibeon (1 Kings 3.4–15) where, at the beginning of his reign, Yahweh likewise allows him a wish, throws a quite appropriate light on this aspect of the court style. The fulfilment of the wish is assured before even the king himself can express it; Yahweh promises him dominion over the nations to the very ends of the earth. The last strophe, following the restoration of the text, has nothing more to say about the king on Zion. It exhorts the kings to serve Yahweh with fear and to kiss his feet with reverence, so that his anger might not blaze out against them. The real theme of this Psalm is clearly the worldwide dominion of Yahweh over the nations. The king on Zion is, because of his dignity as son, the feudal tenant of this dominion. Because of the worldwide dimension in which it is set, this Psalm has something rather unreal about it. To speak of the king of Judah in such terms is really a gross exaggeration. But to speak of Yahweh's dominion in this way is quite in accordance with the Yahweh faith, which becomes ever more fully comprehensible in its encounter with the nations of the world. This Psalm, which speaks of the actual dominion of the king on Zion, thereby takes on a proportion which transcends the bare historical reality. It looks beyond to the as yet outstanding kingdom of God.

One would like to mention Psalm 72 in this context: an introductory petition for the king describes him as the lord who rules the world with complete righteousness; the most distant nations bring him tribute; and under his prosperous rule nature itself produces the finest fruits. One cannot miss the element of transcendence over the empirical world.[4]

Side by side with this we hear in Psalm 89 the agonized voice of the Psalmist in a time of distress as he disputes with Yahweh about the fulfilment of the promise given to David. It is not the voice of the disputant, but the voice of the humble penitent that echoes through the Deuteronomic history which, in the darkness of the exilic period, describes the collapse of the royal house of David which had been maintained and given assurance by so many divine promises. The history closes with the account of the amnesty granted to the descendants of the house of David after thirty-seven years in exile (2 Kings 25.27–30); an overall view of this historical work would not exclude the possibility that this conclusion is quietly putting the question whether Yahweh's promise might not initiate a new and unexpected history for the house of David. This expectation suddenly blazes forth in the proclamation of Haggai and Zechariah in the immediate post-exilic period which seized at once on Zerubbabel of the house of

David, who had been sent by the Persian king to Jerusalem, and saw in him the anointed of Yahweh and the guarantor of a period of prosperity that was imminent for Jerusalem. There are traces of editorial reflection in Zechariah 6.9–15, which originally told of how Zechariah was preparing a crown for Zerubbabel, and of the equally sudden extinction of this hope.

Together with these expressions of hope, which attached themselves to the ruling member of the house of David or to him present in the Persian governor, there is another series of expressions which speak of the hope in the descendant of David, who incorporates the kingdom of Yahweh, and which are clearly opposed to the ruling descendant. This separation of the ruling descendant of David from the real descendant, who is to be expected as the king to come, is to be found in the writings of the great prophets.

It is not clear how one should interpret in detail the disputed text of Amos 9.11–12, in which Yahweh promises to restore the fallen house of David.[5] Only the political aspect of a restoration of the Davidic rule comes through. It is quite different with Isaiah of Jerusalem who among the prophets rightly deserves the title of the herald of the Davidic-Messianic hope. Isaiah 9.6–7 proclaims the new David in expressions which recall Psalm 2; the background is a mighty act of liberation by Yahweh to the advantage of the people who had been trampled on by the Assyrian military boot. According to Albrecht Alt,[6] the writer would be thinking particularly of the provinces of Gilead, Megiddo, and Dor in north Israel which had been cut off in the year 733. It is rather questionable, however, if, as Alt thinks, the writer is thinking of a real change of king in Judah, so that the expectation would hand on a young king actually reigning in Jerusalem. This is not at all the case in Isaiah 11.1ff., where in the oracle about the shoot which is to blossom from the severed trunk of Jesse, the judgement which has already fallen on the royal house cannot be missed. Both of these descriptions of the king of the future are, however, at one in underlining very strongly the element of righteousness which belongs to the king. Isaiah 11.6–8 extends this peace and prosperity in the kingdom of the king to the animal world. The primeval feud between man and beast which the Yahwist spoke of in Genesis 3, and the priestly writer in Genesis 9, will end in the peace of the kingdom.

> Great shall the dominion be,
> and boundless the peace
> bestowed on David's throne and on his kingdom,
> to establish it and sustain it
> with justice and righteousness
> from now and for evermore.
> The zeal of the Lord of Hosts shall do this (9.7).

And Isaiah 11.2–5 speaks in broad outlines of the spirit of Yahweh, the spirit of knowledge and the fear of the Lord, by which the future ruler

> ... shall not judge by what he sees
> nor decide by what he hears;
> he shall judge the poor with justice
> and defend the humble in the land with equity.

The poor and humble will be allowed to have their say, and the unjust will be destroyed.

It would be completely false to see in these oracles mere Utopian dreams or wishful thinking. Just as Yahweh had not allowed the northern neighbours to wantonly set a foreigner on the throne of David in the Syro-Ephraimitic war, so would he also, in accordance with the faith of Isaiah, make good his promise of a righteous king, even though it be accomplished by judgement and devastation. Isaiah and his people, whose destiny lies in the hand of 'the Holy One of Israel', are conscious that they are advancing towards the future of such a righteous kingdom.

This is also the proclamation in the prophecy about the time to come. Jeremiah 23.1ff., looking at the events in critical perspective, opposes the 'righteous branch from David's line' to the shepherds who lead astray and scatter Yahweh's flock. This righteous branch will be

> a king who shall rule wisely,
> maintaining law and justice in the land.
> In his days Judah shall be kept safe,
> and Israel shall live undisturbed.
> This is the name to be given to him:
> the Lord is our Righteousness.

Whatever judgement one may pronounce on this oracle of Jeremiah, it is clear that Yahweh's king, who carries by right the name 'the Lord is our Salvation/Righteousness', is being contrasted with the last king of Judah, the weak, but not wicked, Zedekiah, whose name means 'Yahweh is my Salvation/ Righteousness'. Ezekiel 34, with its quite lengthy polemic against the wicked shepherds and its announcement of the good shepherd, is in the same line. But here it is no longer the king whose name is a counterbalance to that of Zedekiah that is expected; it is a new David, opening up the vistas of Yahweh's original plan for salvation: 'He shall care for them and become their shepherd. I, the Lord, will become their God . . .' (34.23). What is expressed here quite clearly is that with the king to come it is not a question of a man, but of God's reign. Nor is it a question of a vision in the sky, but of peace and justice on earth:

> Now I myself will judge between the fat sheep and the lean. You hustle the weary with flank and shoulder, you butt them with your horns until you have driven them away and scattered them abroad. Therefore I will save my flock, and they shall be ravaged no more; I will judge between one sheep and another.[7]

Zechariah 9.9–10 is a witness of how the qualities of humility and the removal of military might are mingled in the expectation of the one who is to come:

> Rejoice, rejoice, daughter of Zion,
> shout aloud, daughter of Jerusalem;
> for see, your king is coming to you,
> his cause won, his victory gained,
> humble and mounted on an ass,
> on a foal, the young of a she-ass.
> He shall banish chariots from Ephraim[8]
> and war-horses from Jerusalem;
> the warrior's bow shall be banished.
> He shall speak peaceably to every nation,
> and his rule shall extend from sea to sea,
> from the River to the ends of the earth.

The New Testament form of address, 'Son of David', is a clear proof that these hopes were not completely extinguished.[9]

It would be very one-sided, however, if one were to consider Israel's hope for the future only from the standpoint of royal Messianism. This hope is articulated in quite different ways.[10] Part of the acceptance which Israel has received from her God is the promise of his nearness, his presence in the midst of his people. Old Testament faith knows that it is in the place of his presence that it receives the gift of life, as we have already seen in detail in the previous chapter. The hope of Old Testament faith can look also to the sanctuary. There is a promise of salvation in Isaiah 2.2–4 which is also taken up by Isaiah's contemporary, Micah (4.1–3); though the oracle may originate with neither of these prophets, it would certainly come from the war-torn Assyrian period. There is a description of the great pilgrimage of the nations to the mountain of God in Jerusalem with the central purpose of world peace and world disarmament.

> In days to come
> the mountain of the Lord's house
> shall be set over all other mountains,
> lifted high above the hills.
> All the nations shall come streaming to it,
> and many peoples shall come and say,
> 'Come, let us climb up on the mountain of the Lord,
> to the house of the god of Jacob,
> that he may teach us his ways
> and we may walk in his paths.'
> For instruction issues from Zion,
> and out of Jerusalem comes the word of the Lord;
> he will be judge between nations,
> arbiter among many peoples.
> They shall beat their swords into mattocks
> and their spears into pruning-knives;
> nation shall not lift sword against nation
> nor ever again be trained for war.

What is to be brought about by the king of peace in Zechariah 9.9ff. is here the direct effect of God's instruction given at the place of his presence, where all the nations have gathered. No other prophetic oracle which speaks of the pilgrimage to Zion contains such an intense hope for Yahweh's peace. Haggai 2.7, at a time when the temple lies in ruins, expects that the nations will confer on it a new glory with their gifts. The temple is included in the broader context of the new city and its glory, over which the light of Yahweh will shine after the period of privation. The city and the temple will be rebuilt in new glory by the gifts of the people who flock to it, and Yahweh will be honoured by the glory of the new city which will be called 'the Zion of the Holy One of Israel' (Isa. 60).

The priestly vision of the future contains no expectation of a pilgrimage of the nations (Ezek. 40ff.). Here the temple, built in magnificent symmetry, stands alone on the high mountain.[11] Here the unprecedented happens: Yahweh resumes his dwelling place in all his glory (41.1ff.). God's saving action is to be recognized in the stream of water; from insignificant beginnings it swells into a mighty river and flows from the middle of the temple out into the land, giving life again to the Dead Sea, long lifeless from an ancient curse (47.1–12).

In all these expectations the Davidic king has retreated completely behind Yahweh and his divine presence. A further variation of the hope of Israel is to be found in Deutero-Isaiah, who now extends the ancient promise to David to the whole people and at the same time sees the saving action that is taking place there in the broader perspective of the nations:

I will make a covenant with you, this time for ever,
to love you faithfully as I loved David.
I made him a witness to all races,
a prince and instructor of peoples;
and you in turn shall summon nations you do not know,
and nations that do not know you shall come running to you,
because the Lord your God,
the Holy One of Israel, has glorified you (Isa. 55.3–5).

There is no sign here of a Messianic ruler from the house of David; as Isaiah 45.1 can show, the title of the anointed is given to the foreign, heathen prince Cyrus, who is thereby empowered to guarantee freedom to Israel as she sits in banishment and enable her to return to the land. This final perspective of the hope of Deutero-Isaiah consists in something much greater than political power. It is a question of Yahweh becoming known throughout the world through the action whereby he liberates his people yet again. Just as the kingdom of David acted as a witness for Yahweh among the nations of the world, so now the newly restored and favoured people is to be a witness to the nations among whom it is dispersed, and far beyond the confines of its immediate surroundings.

The acceptance which Israel experienced from the very begin-

ning of her history in the action of her God, becomes here an instrument in respect of a much wider acceptance which Yahweh
addresses to all nations. Israel, Yahweh's witness, becomes
Yahweh's servant in the service of the worldwide intention of
Yahweh, which can be seen in the oath of Isaiah 45.22ff.:

> Look to me and be saved,
> you peoples from all corners of the earth;
> for I am God, there is no other.
> By my life I have sworn,
> I have given a promise of victory,
> a promise that will not be broken,
> that to me every knee shall bend
> and by me every tongue shall swear.
> In the Lord alone, men shall say,[12]
> are victory and might;
> and all who defy him[13]
> shall stand ashamed in his presence,
> but all the sons of Israel shall stand victorious
> and find their glory in the Lord.

It is not the place here to address oneself to the complex
problem of the 'servant of Yahweh' which arises in Deutero-
Isaiah, and which can scarcely be limited to the people of Israel.[14]
It must suffice here to make one point: the oracles of the servant
open Israel completely to the nations. And it becomes clear that
the ultimate perspective of the hope of Israel embraces the nations
who will recognize how unreserved are the compassion and the
saving will of this God who calls again to glory the people whom
he had shattered because of their guilt.

Something must be said here about the hope of the successors
of the prophets, who speak in the apocalyptic writings of the Old
Testament.[15] Here it is no longer a question of the expectation of
the pilgrimage to God's mountain in Israel, nor of the idea of the
proclamation of Yahweh's acts among the Gentiles. The concern
is concentrated rather on the last decisive crisis from which
Yahweh emerges with the definitive establishment of his kingdom
and rule. The details are expressed in a very different sort of
vocabulary.

The prophecy about Gog and Magog in Ezekiel 38–9, a
forerunner of the apocalyptic thinking, looks to a decisive battle in

the land of Israel which annihilates the enemy hordes and brings definitive peace to God's people.[16] According to Joel a great judgement of the nations will take place in the valley of Jehosophat, which will occur after Israel has returned to her God in penance.[17] The fullest and most clearly localized apocalyptic book of the Old Testament is the book of Daniel. It grew to its final form in the white heat of a new attack on the people of God by the Seleucid king, Antiochus Epiphanes. Nebuchadnezzar's dream of the huge image (ch. 2) which was shattered by a stone hewn from a mountain, not by human hands, shows how the world empires will be destroyed by God in the final crisis to make way for his kingdom. Chapter 7 portrays these world empires by means of ever more gruesome animals. The human form descends from heaven, passes sober judgement on the beasts, and receives the sovereignty; this human form, which stands for the people, the saints of the most high,[18] is promised victory by God. It is not without opposition, but through the crisis of a final world judgement that God ultimately effects his kingdom, which is now present in his people in the world.

The realization of justice between men, the restoration of a state of peace in which no one carries arms, these no longer occur in the apocalyptic sketches. Something quite new breaks through in the framework of the expectation of this last world crisis. In the final great affliction, when the last great enemy falls, then it will happen:

> At that moment Michael shall appear, Michael the great captain,
> who stands guard over your fellow-countrymen;
> and there will be a time of distress
> such as has never been
> since they became a nation till that moment.
> But at that moment your people will be delivered,
> every one who is written in the book:
> many of those who sleep in the dust of the earth will wake,
> some to everlasting life
> and some to the reproach of eternal abhorrence.
> The wise leaders shall shine like the bright vault of heaven,
> and those who have guided the people in the true path
> shall be like the stars for ever and ever (Dan. 12.1–3).

A barrier is breached here, the barrier of death, before which the faith of Israel stops firm and fast, as was established in the discussion of life and death in the Old Testament. Has this late representative of Old Testament faith finally capitulated before the divinities of the surrounding world? To pass judgement on this question we must examine carefully the point at which this breach with the older belief took place. There is no trace here of a god like Osiris, Tammuz, or Adonis. The starting point of belief in life after death is sharp opposition to the attacks of a foreign faith; the community of the God of Israel has been besieged and has sealed the siege with martyrdom. There is nothing at all here of that tendency to follow Baal, characteristic of the time before King Josiah, when the God of Israel was likened to a foreign god who gave people access to rights which would assure them of life beyond death. There is not a trace of such rights, and they are *a priori* quite improbable. In addition, hope in some wakening from the dead breaks through where God's righteousness is active. In the period of persecution those who were loyal adhered to God. Those who were not turned from him. The faithful lost their lives in this religious struggle; the faithless apparently preserved their lives so as to be able to bring them to the close of their natural cycle. In the midst of this, where is God's acceptance of his people?

Hope of an awakening from the dead opens up with the question of God's righteousness with respect to his people. The older faith of Israel would have seen God's righteousness of his acceptance of his people hidden in the promise that Israel would continue to live. The vision in which the dead bones are called to life again (Ezek. 37) is a promise that the house of Israel as a whole will continue to live. In this late period, when a demand in faith is made on each individual by way of persecution, this assurance no longer carries weight, especially in face of God's definitive decision with regard to his people. It was here that the belief was awakened that God would pass judgement also on the individual: the faithful would have life, and the unfaithful destruction. It is significant, however, that nothing is said here of an actual resurrection of the individual; but that the event embraces the individual in God's definitive act of salvation towards the community as a whole.

Related to these, but with quite different and individual marks of their own, are the oracles about victory over death in what is known as the Apocalypse of Isaiah (Isa. 24—7), a somewhat older work. In the background is the proclamation of a great, final world judgement (24.1ff.), in which Yahweh's final decisions come upon the world and in which the history of the nations comes to the end intended by God. As in the older prophecies, this decision is bound to the place where Yahweh is present among his people. Instead of a great pilgrimage of the nations there is a banquet for them on the mountain, where Yahweh's final decisions take effect:

> On this mountain the Lord of Hosts will prepare
> a banquet of rich fare for all the peoples,
> a banquet of wines well matured and richest fare,
> well-matured wines strained clear.
> On this mountain the Lord will swallow up
> that veil that shrouds all the peoples,
> the pall thrown over all the nations;
> he will swallow up death for ever.
> Then the Lord God will wipe away the tears from every face
> and remove the reproach of his people from the whole earth.
> The Lord has spoken (Isa. 25.6–8).

The isolated passage from Isaiah 26.19 should be considered in this context:

> But thy dead live, their bodies will rise again.[19]
> They that sleep in the earth will awake and shout for joy;[20]
> for thy dew is a dew of sparkling light,
> and the earth will bring those long dead to birth again.

Though the second citation is not altogether clear, the first recalls Exodus 24.9–11, where the God of Israel invited the representatives of the people to a covenant meal on God's mountain in the desert. So when everything is to be finally sealed, the nations of the world are to be invited to an unusual covenant meal, where all life's cares are to be done away with, those which had been mentioned in part in the paradise story in Genesis 3: pain and death. The removal of the veil, contrary to the interpretation most favoured today, which sees in it the removal of mourning clothes, could well refer to the removal of the persistent blindness of the eyes before the real Lord of the world. With the acknowledgement of Yahweh as the unique Lord of the world, Israel's humiliation and mistake are removed.

It is not so much the thought of Yahweh in his righteousness making a final judgement that is at the centre, but rather faith in the final fulfilment of the concern of the creator for his world. One can see, too, God's final word of acceptance to the nations which had already been proclaimed by Deutero-Isaiah.

In this context we must refer back again to what the last passage had to say about life and death, because it is quite possible to see the beginnings of a radical hope for life beyond death in some of the Psalms and in the book of Job. We must try to determine precisely where this hope began, because it is something different from the hope which Israel's neighbours had of regaining life after death.

When speaking of the Psalms we noticed how passionately the Psalmist spoke out against his enemies and disputed to gain acknowledgement of his own righteousness. Behind this lay hidden the struggle for God's gracious glance, the evidence of which was found in the promise of life in the practical outcome of the present. The problem of the misfortune of the good and the prosperity of the wicked became here ever more and more acute. It was not only Qoheleth (Ecclesiastes) who considered this within the framework of his biting and rather sober observations on life. Jeremiah too in his confessions was sensitive to the lot of the prophet in the face of this mystery which he experienced personally, e.g. Jeremiah 12.1ff. We come across reflection on this problem in a Wisdom Psalm, Psalm 73. The Psalmist confesses that he had almost come to grief on this question. But then in God's sanctuary the scales fell from his eyes. Unfortunately we have no further details of what caused his change of attitude. But the result is clear. With quite daring confidence the Psalmist confesses that he knows that God has put the godless on slippery ground, yet confesses to his own profit, and entrusts himself unconditionally to his God:

> Yet I am always with thee,
> thou holdest my right hand;
> thou dost guide me by thy counsel
> and afterwards wilt receive me with glory.
> Whom have I in heaven but thee?
> And having thee, I desire nothing else on earth.
> Though heart and body fail,
> yet God is my possession for ever (Ps. 73.24–6).

The Psalmist uses the verb 'take away' which also occurs in the narrative of the taking away of Henoch and Elijah.[21] But there are no further details. It can, however, scarcely be denied that the Psalmist, when speaking of his being hidden from the hand of God, who snatches him away, is looking to something beyond. This again is something completely different from the Canaanite belief in a coming to life again which was spoken about in analogies taken from nature. Everything depends on the fidelity of the word of Yahweh, who has spoken his acceptance even to the individual members of his people.

It is even clearer in the book of Job, where a pious man who has experienced the extremes of life fights his way through the affliction of abandonment by God. The affliction is made even more acute because his friends take a stand against him, and, against all evidence, champion more and more the cause that evil comes only on the wicked. Job struggles against this in defence of the integrity of God who has spoken his approval to him, because Job stands by him. It becomes ever more clear that he is grappling with the justice that God has spoken to him and is crying out for a confirmation of this from God. Using the categories of the court he appeals to the witness whom he has in God, to stand by him against his friends and against their god (16.18–21). Finally he uses the categories of blood vengeance, the custom according to which the next of kin is obliged to avenge the blood of the victim on the murderer. He takes into account that his death is sealed. At the same time, however, he reaches beyond death:

> For I know that my Redeemer lives,
> and at last he will stand upon the earth;
> and after my skin has been thus destroyed,
> then without my flesh I shall see God (19.25–6, RSV).[22]

Once more the imagery gives us no light. Job's world picture does not include the 'beyond'. But what he passionately confesses is that he has a God who stands by him, and that he will see him again.

These last two passages are not dealing with the matter of the apocalyptic writings, namely with a great event which concerns the world and the nations, in which Yahweh speaks his final acceptance to his people and beyond them to the nations, as well as speaking his rejection to the world of death. It is an individual who is speaking here. He is certain that he has heard God's acceptance (cf. Ps. 73.16–17); with confidence in this acceptance, he ventures to hope beyond death.

In all this has Old Testament faith abandoned the world and arrived at a belief which takes a stand on the 'beyond'? An overall view of these different expressions of hope, even of those which burst the limits of a life bound by death, should have made it clear that this world is in no wise sacrificed. Even the hope which seems to burst the boundaries of death is directed to the world, to the fidelity of God to the world that he has created, and to the people that he has called there. In any case all these expressions of hope look to the coming of something new, to a world which has been promised God's saving action, and which faith advances to meet in hope. This expectation is expressed in its most all-embracing form in the promise of the third part of the book of Isaiah:

> For behold, I create
> new heavens and a new earth.
> Former things shall no more be remembered
> nor shall they be called to mind.
> Rejoice and be filled with delight,
> you boundless realms which I create;
> for I create Jerusalem to be a delight
> and her people a joy;
> I will take delight in Jerusalem and rejoice in my people;
> weeping and cries for help
> shall never again be heard in her (65.17–19).

The speaker is not concerned with a heaven beyond or with a paradise beyond, but with something quite new that Yahweh has in mind for his world, for Jerusalem, and for his people. Old Testament hope is hope for the world.

11

THE OLD TESTAMENT
AND THE WORLD:
LAW OR GOSPEL?

(Bultmann's essay 'Prophecy and Fulfilment' may be found in *Essays on Old Testament Interpretation*, ed. Claus Westermann, English trans. ed. L. L. Mays, London: SCM Press (1963), pp. 50–75. The passages cited in this chapter have been rendered by the present translator.)

We saw in the first chapter that the Old Testament, with its striking and carefree implication in the world, early became an object of suspicion to the Christian faith. We saw too how this suspicion has persisted alive right up to the present day. Rudolph Bultmann, in his significant essay 'Prophecy and Fulfilment', raised the question to what extent is Jewish Old Testament history prophecy, which is fulfilled in the history of the New Testament community. His answer is that the Old Testament can be prophecy only in its 'failure'.[1] Having gone through the Old Testament and considered the different aspects of its relationship to the world, we must now confront this question which the New Testament has put to the Old Testament, and inquire if it is justified.

Bultmann first of all examines the prophecies of fulfilment which are found in the New Testament, and the method by which the New Testament used passages from the Old to confirm New Testament events. He maintains that this is not possible for an age which thinks in historical-critical categories. He then takes issue with the work of J. C. K. Hoffmann, *Prophecy and Fulfilment* (1841–4), which is concerned not with Old Testament prophecies, but with the history to which the Old Testament gives witness and which it understands as prophecy. This history, as it moves towards its goal, carries its goal within it as prophecy or promise. Bultmann first points out that behind this mentality

137

there is a philosophy of history coloured and influenced by Hegel, the theological relevance of which for the meaning of Christ is not at all clear. He then asks further whether there is not nevertheless something correct in the way Hoffmann has put the question: is the Old Testament history to be understood as prophecy from its consummation in Christ? This is the transition point to the important discussions of three areas of Old Testament thought concerning which Bultmann now develops his views.

First there is the idea of the covenant which in ancient times was understood as a real bond between God and the Israel of history. It was sealed by sacrifice, it was maintained by sacrifice. On the other hand there arose the prophetic proclamation which in the first place protested against the binding of God to the land. This proclamation also made the validity of the covenant dependent on the people's obedience. A covenant with a people which would be founded on the fulfilment of certain moral demands as a condition of the covenant is, as an historical reality, an impossibility. It is the individual who must ultimately show obedience. Consequently God's covenant with a people whose individual members are to be but units of a people under a moral demand from God, becomes an eschatological notion, because such a people has an eschatological, and not an empirical, historical, dimension. This becomes quite clear in the expectation expressed by the prophet Jeremiah (31.31ff.). The New Testament resumes this outlook when it speaks of the new covenant and sees it fulfilled in the community of Christ, inasmuch as it understands it in a radically eschatological sense. 'The new covenant has a radical, eschatological dimension, i.e. a dimension beyond the world, and the fact of belonging to it removes its adherents from the world' (Bultmann).[2] Circumcision as the sign of the covenant drops out, just as does the separation of the people of the covenant from other nations. Something similar is to be said of the idea of the kingship of God. The kingship too is understood in the New Testament in a quite realistic way as a kingship over Israel, which is recognizable in the concurrence of the divine and the earthly kingdoms. The kingship of Yahweh was celebrated in the feast of the enthronement, and it was experienced there by the pious community. This rule developed into an eschatological expectation, particularly in the period of the exile. In the postexilic period, descriptions of the present and future kingships go side by side. The apocalyptic writers expect that the kingship of God will burst in like a new era together with the world judgement. This is the point of contact with the New Testament, which understands the existence of the community, now loosened from the ancient community, as the realization of God's reign. The community is understood as having at the same time a dimension within and outside the world:

> The rule of God, that is of Christ, is therefore something completely different from what the Old Testament prophets had expected. It is completely eschatological and beyond the world; and the person who shares in it is likewise removed from the world, so that though still 'in the flesh', he nevertheless no longer lives 'according to the flesh' (2 Cor. 10.3).[3]

The inconsistency of Paul, who divides the eschatological event into the present and the future, is overcome completely by John inasmuch as he makes everything present. We hear from the lips of Christ: 'My kingdom does not belong to this world' (1 John 18.36).

> That Jesus has overcome the world (1 John 16.33) is not perceptible within the world, but shows itself in this, that the world remains given over to itself. But the victory of Jesus continues in the victory of faith over the world (1 John 5.3) (Bultmann).[4]

Thirdly there is the idea of the people of God. One can establish early in the Old Testament the inner tension between the idea of the people of God and the kingdom of the world. This tension is clearly perceptible in the prophetic demands for the political mobilization of the kings: 'Where their ideals lead to a legal code, the resulting outline is a Utopia.'[5] This can be seen both in Deuteronomy and in the priestly writings. But in the post-exilic attempt to live as a theocracy under foreign rule, Judaism, which wants to be at the same time God's people and a natural community, remains a self-contradiction. The Messiah, expected now here now there, remains a shadow-like figure. The situation becomes clear in the New Testament, inasmuch as the people of God present in the Christian community has no more an empirical, historical dimension. 'It does not exist as a people that needs organization and institutions. The state therefore, in so far as it is really a state, i.e. a system of law, is rendered ineffective

(Rom. 13); it is, so to speak, removed from the sphere of interest of the people of God (1 Cor. 6.1ff.)' (Bultmann).[6]

The basis is now laid for Bultmann to draw his final conclusions. The Old Testament history of Judaism lives in a profound internal contradiction. 'The contradiction consists in this, that God and his action are not understood in the radically eschatological and transcendent sense, but are to be brought under the cover of the empirical history of the people. It is on this contradiction that history founders.'[7]

But according to Bultmann Old Testament promise is resolved in the very event on which it founders. Of fulfilment in Christ, the following can be said:

> For man, promise can be nothing else than the failure of his method, than the acknowledgement of the impossibility of taking hold of God directly in his historical action within the world, or of identifying the world's own internal history directly with the action of God.[8]

And so Old Testament history comes to the place where the 'contradiction which is peculiar to human existence as such' becomes clear: 'To be created for God, to be called to God, and yet to be hamstrung by the history of the world.'[9]

Bultmann believes that he is thereby following the Pauline interpretation of the law. The law leads to a foundering on sin—but this is the way to faith.

> In order to be certain of itself faith needs knowledge of the meaning of the law; otherwise it would be constantly open to seduction by the law, whatever form this may take. Faith likewise needs to look back into Old Testament history as a history of failure, and so of promise, so as to know that the state of one who has been justified is raised up on the foundation of failure. Just as faith constantly carries within it the vanquished path of the law in order really to be a faith of justification, so also it constantly carries within it the vanquished attempt to identify the worldly and the eschatological, in order to be of an eschatological nature.[10]

It can be said of this eschatological life that it plays itself out 'in the moment, in the individual', which is then described, by an extraordinary narrowing of the term, as 'the sphere of history'.[11]

Bultmann's view is clear in outline: the Old Testament links the most fundamental expressions of religion to the people of Israel as a recognizable and defined unit within the world. But the Old Testament itself makes it clear that such a simplified approach to the reality of history cannot stand. It begins to eschatologize the promises without freeing them entirely from Israel. The failure of this form of belief is already proclaimed in the Old Testament, a failure that is completely confirmed by New Testament faith, in which there enter, in place of the Old Testament setting within the world, the basic realities which are not of this world, namely Christ and his community. This foundering is to be set side by side with man's foundering on law. It is only in a radical and eschatological dissociation from the world, which has renounced law, that faith can really be faith.

Behind this view there is a definite equation: occupation with the world, faith bound to historical phenomena within the world, correspond to existence under the law. Faith, understood biblically, means eschatological life outside the confines of the world, freedom from occupation with the world.

If one asks after the basis of this equation, Bultmann will refer to those passages of John which speak of the world. 'The victory is mine; I have conquered the world.'[12] 'The victory that defeats the world is our faith.'[13] But two questions arise here: is the notion of the world, which through the whole of the Old Testament is linked with expressions of Old Testament faith, to be equated with what is described as the 'world' in the Johannine writings? And secondly: this judgement of the Old Testament as law, based on this equation, and which leads to a foundering of human existence, is it really valid?

We can begin with the second question. The Old Testament does indeed speak of a foundering (failure) of Israel. Its rumblings begin very early in the history of the wandering in the desert of the people liberated from Egypt. Israel had committed the outrage of the golden calf, violating the second commandment which demanded that she should worship without any image; immediately following this, Exodus 32.9ff. reports the angry words of God to Moses:

> I have considered this people, and I see that they are a stubborn people. Now, let me alone to vent my anger upon them, so that I may put an end to them and make a great nation spring from you.

It was only with difficulty that Moses' intercession succeeded and prevented the people from being annihilated. Again there is the story of the scouts who were sent to explore the land: they brought back reports of the strongly fortified cities in the land which was to be conquered, and the people lost courage when they heard the news. They would not enter the land and they turned against God whose will it was to lead them and give them his victory. Yahweh's anger blazed out once more:

> How much longer will this people treat me with contempt? How much longer will they refuse to trust me in spite of all the signs I have shown among them? I will strike them with pestilence. I will deny them their heritage, and you and your descendants I will make into a nation greater and more numerous than they (Num. 14.11ff.).

The people again becomes hard in face of its failure and is only saved by Moses' renewed intercession.

What is told here by way of projection back into the history of the beginning, comes right to the fore in the clear light of historical reality in the proclamation of the great pre-exilic prophets and in the history which gave rise to this proclamation. We hear the harsh attacks of the prophets on a people that will neither listen to nor follow Yahweh's command:

> There is no good faith or mutual trust,
> no knowledge of God in the land,
> oaths are imposed and broken, they kill and rob;
> there is nothing but adultery and licence,
> one deed of blood after another.
> Therefore the land shall be dried up,
> and all who live in it shall pine away ... (Hos. 4.1–3).

These words are spoken by Hosea to the northern kingdom. And Micah has this to say of the leaders in Judah:

> Listen to this, leaders of Jacob,
> rulers of Israel,
> you who make justice hateful
> and wrest it from its straight course,
> building Zion in bloodshed
> and Jerusalem in iniquity.
> Her rulers sell justice,
> her priests give direction in return for a bribe,
> her prophets take money for their divination,
> and yet men rely on the Lord.

'Is not the Lord among us?' they say;
'then no disaster can befall us.'
Therefore, on your account
Zion shall become a ploughed field,
Jerusalem a heap of ruins,
and the temple hill rough heath (3.9–12).

The complaint of Jeremiah in his temple sermon 100 years later is almost the same:

> You steal, you murder, you commit adultery and perjury, you burn sacrifices to Baal, you run after other gods whom you have not known; then you come and stand before me in this house, which bears my name, and say, 'We are safe' (7.9ff.).

On the basis of this accusation, he pronounces against the temple in Jerusalem the fate which befell the shrine at Shiloh some hundreds of years before. One could also allege the graphic description of Ezekiel 22.6ff., where the prophet as it were ticks off with his finger a whole list of commandments, and demonstrates in each case that leaders of the people have flagrantly violated them, and that for this reason the people will be dispersed throughout the pagan world.

Israel's failure in the matter of the commandments is graphically demonstrated in these cases, and the subsequent history has vividly confirmed what was announced there. There is no sign at all that the prophets protested specifically against the bond between the people and the land, and thereby showed the way to Bultmann's New Testament 'un-preoccupation with the world'. The bond with the land is the datum which is taken for granted; the loss of the land is that form of the divine judgement which demonstrates Israel's failure. The failure occurs not because of the bond with the land, but because of the actual transgression of commandments given to the people. It occurs because the people breaks away from God's leadership and refuses to follow him.

The question arises in all this as to whether Bultmann does not render sin ineffectual when he sees it included predominantly in the world concern of Old Testament faith. The view of the prophets was that real obedience belonged truly to the world, inasmuch as marriage was highly regarded, the property and life of one's neighbour were respected, the truth was spoken, an oath was kept, justice was done, and in all this God was properly honoured.

The rescue of the people from their failure takes place in close association with the land. Ezekiel 37.1ff., in the imagery of the dead bones called to life, describes how Israel is to be restored to the land. And the same Ezekiel announces with inexorable rigour that this new beginning is not to happen because of any vestige of good that may still have remained in Israel, but only because of God's zeal for the honour of his name:

> It is not for your sake, you Israelites, that I am acting, but for the sake of my holy name, which you have profaned among the peoples where you have gone. I will hallow my great name, which has been profaned among those nations. . . . I will take you out of the nations and gather you from every land and bring you to your own soil. I will sprinkle clean water over you, and you shall be cleansed from all that defiles you . . . (36.22–4).[14]

That other great prophet of the later exile, Deutero-Isaiah, who has been called the evangelist of the Old Testament, says just the same thing, though spiritually he comes from a quite different circle. From the abyss of Israel's failure, which is wide open to the whole world, he proclaims with consummate joy the imminent rescue and the return to the land. He does it with brilliant colours in an eschatology of his own, which sees the whole world in movement.[15] Central to his proclamation is the capital message: you are to return home to the land. God speaks his acceptance again to those who have failed. He too declares definitively that this is to take place not because of any merit at all of the people:

> Yet you did not call upon me, O Jacob;
> much less did you weary yourself in my service, O Israel.
> You did not bring me sheep as whole-offerings
>
> . . .
>
> or glut me with the fat of your sacrifices;
> rather you burdened me with your sins
> and wearied me with your iniquities.
> I alone, I am He,
> who for his own sake wipes out your transgressions,
> who will remember your sins no more.
> Cite me by name, let us argue it out;

> set forth your pleading and justify yourselves.
> Your first father transgressed,
> your spokesman rebelled against me,
> . . .
> so I sent Jacob to his doom
> and left Israel to execration (Isa. 43.22–8).

Is it mere chance that with this message of unmerited, free grace, a grace which Yahweh allows out of compassion rather than justice, the gates are opened to the nations, and that here, where the granting of grace is so extraordinary, there comes into the field of vision a world also called by God? Israel, a people blind and deaf, which has still not understood Yahweh's ways, and over whom Yahweh's great saving action is now breaking, is to become his witness among the nations and through what it has experienced, to make Yahweh's honour great among them, so that the heathen will come and bow the knee before Yahweh.

This charge, of bringing God's extraordinary grace-giving decision to the nations, is fully described in the songs of the servant of Yahweh:

> He will not break a bruised reed,
> or snuff out a smouldering wick;
> he will make justice shine on every race,
> never faltering, never breaking down,
> he will plant justice on earth,
> while coasts and islands wait for his teaching (Isa. 42.3–4).

Later Yahweh addresses directly the servant:

> It is too slight a task for you, as my servant,
> to restore the tribes of Jacob,
> to bring back the descendants of Israel:
> I will make you a light to the nations,
> to be my salvation to earth's farthest bounds (49.6).

These songs lead up to that final and most mysterious account of the servant, who is plunged into the deepest suffering, even into death, and has borne this burden for others: 'He bore the sin of many and interceded for their transgressions' (Isa. 53.12).

It cannot go unnoticed that here at the very centre of the Old Testament there is an account of the utter failure of Yahweh's people and of its completely undeserved restoration, and that the

saving action of God which Deutero-Isaiah proclaims will cast its
light far among the nations. It is just as clear that this is not portrayed as an empty hope for the future, unsupported by any
historical event; the historical support did eventuate, on however
less spectacular and more modest a scale than the two prophets of
the exile may have expected. Israel foundered, but did not perish.
She experienced a corporal restoration and, however changed its
external form, was given new life in the land.

One must ask Bultmann: is the whole of this Old Testament
event, including the restoration of the defunct people after the
exile, merely a foundering on the law? Is there not something
quite different here? And further, one must ask again with a certain insistence whether sin is not rendered ineffectual, when the
real place where Israel foundered on the law is thought to be concern for the world of her belief, and where redemption of the
sinner from sin consists in concern for the world being divested of
the world, and what is within the world moving beyond the world.

This forces us to look at the Christian proclamation where, according to Bultmann, this takes place. Certainly, when Christ,
whom the community confesses as the Son of God, dies on the
cross for the guilt of the world, something quite radical takes place
that leaves the Old Testament message far behind. But does what
is radical in the New Testament really consist in leaving behind
definitively the concern for the world (the worldly) and passing
over to the non-worldly? Is the 'law' on which the world founders
before the cross, really the law which concerns the world (the law
of the worldly)? Is it such that in it it would become clear what
Israel's state was under the law, when it heard and experienced
the proclamation of Deutero-Isaiah, that the great message of
God's merciful and justifying action in favouring his people is to
be carried throughout the whole world?

Does not this foundering of mankind before the cross consist in
something else? Is it not that there is revealed here how mankind
could not bear the overpowering compassion of God, which was
there in Christ for tax-gatherer and sinner, and which did not
break the bruised reed nor snuff out the smouldering wick? Is it
merely that some law of eschatological other-worldliness, basically quite formal, yet formulated without flesh and blood, was set up
to confront man and that it caused him to founder? Was it not
rather the law of perfect love incarnate in the world on which man

foundered? And did not God's acceptance ring out loudly in the Easter event, an acceptance which sent his love fully and incarnate into the world? It was before this gift which shamed Jew and Greek alike that the barriers of a special people of God have fallen. The Israel that went out into the pagan world in the person of the Israelite Paul, invited the world of the Greeks to come under its old, worldwide, limitless promise, now revolutionized in Christ. The strange branch of the pagan world is, as Romans 11.17ff. says, grafted on to the ancient root.

'God loved the world so much that he gave his only son, that everyone who has faith in him may not die but have eternal life'; we read this in that same gospel of 1 John 3.16. It is a stern admonition about the world. Nothing at all is said here about leaving the world behind; it concerns the sending of the Son into the world so that the love of the Father may be there. It is a love which, though not having its origin in the world, is nevertheless incarnate in the world. The Gospel of Mark shows the pre-Easter Christ as the helper and healer of the sick, the feeder of the hungry, the table companion of sinners and tax-collectors in the midst of the world; has Mark so utterly misunderstood the message of Christ as to present him, not only as one who did not stand back critically from the living world, but as giving himself fully to it? Is there really the great gap, where men have foundered utterly on the law, between Christ's life in the world and the Old Testament concern for the world?

This brings us at once to the other question which has arisen in confrontation with the Bultmannian view of the unworldliness effected by the message of Christ, and the foundering of the Old Testament concern with the world. It is the question, whether the critical Johannine view of the cosmos can contribute so simply to a knowledge of the Old Testament meaning of concern with the world (worldliness).

There must be no mistaking that the critical attitude in the Gospel of John acknowledges in the cosmos a domain of inherent power. It is the world that belongs to the law of sin and is an area determined and dominated by it. It is under the dictate of sin that the world does not receive him who comes into it as into his own. The Old Testament is of course quite familiar with what it means to be at enmity with God. Genesis 3, with its account of the beginnings of mankind, has presented it in masterly fashion. The Old

Testament is familiar with the snowballing of evil and man's foundering in it. But at the same time there is a great deal else in the Old Testament. It is striking that the Old Testament proclaims 'the world' not only as the domain of evil, but also describes the lord-like intervention of God in the world, which robs the world of its power. A people is present there which, in accordance with the word of the one who has called it, does not belong to itself and cannot be self-sufficient in its own enclosed system. The power of fertility was given it, but not to be shaped to fit the self-reliant system of the god Eros. Provision was made for the power of man over the world, a power which was not to be exercised like that of God. Victory was given it, but to be accepted as a gift. Land was given, but to be held in trust as a sacred sign. Life and righteousness were on display as gifts bestowed by another, and which were not meant to become entrenched within the walls of a religion of eternal return and renewal or within the confines of a satisfied self-righteousness.

The Old Testament all along the line says that it is this that is taking place in the world, and that man who is taken up into such divine action must open himself to be part of this strange belonging; and this he must do in the very midst of his life in the world, with the people and with his neighbour. The Old Testament has an unusually sharp sensitivity to all those areas where the cosmos would try to make itself independent in a self-contained system of its own against God, be it in the matter of property, political and military power, or even liturgical piety. But it does not proclaim the world of 'the prince of the world'. It proclaims the world of God, who calls his people to himself, and in the people, which is deaf, blind, continually failing, builds his bulwark against the world.

Seen from the standpoint of the New Testament, all this takes place in a forecourt of its own which has no knowledge of that most radical of events before which the whole world will be summoned to make its decision. It is only in the coming of his Son that it becomes clear how much God has loved the world; before this Son the prerogative of a people set apart because of its origin must definitively recede. But it is in the Son that God's concern for the world achieves its fullness. In him there begins to shine much of what was acknowledged in the Old Testament with the coming of God into the affairs of the world.

Is then the Old Testament to be looked on as law or as gospel?
The dialectic of these two areas opens up fully only in the presence
of the Son. The Old Testament lives in a forecourt of its own. It is
not appropriate to subsume the Old Testament under the idea of
law. It is a quite inadmissible exclusion of the most central asser-
tions of the book to subsume the whole of the Old Testament under the perspective of law, especially in the face of all that takes
place in God's intervention to liberate those in bondage and to
restore those who have come to grief on God's command.

On the other hand it is not proper to describe the Old Testament globally as a book of the good news.[16] When this good news
is heard from the standpoint of the cross of Christ, there appears
much in the Old Testament that is quite shocking. The zealous
God of the commandments and of the consuming fire can also
have a counterpart in the zeal of the pious which curses its
enemies; it is not yet complete, as the one who is zealous for mercy
reveals. One may not abolish by decree this Old Testament
characteristic of the still open forecourt. The decisive question
comes in Christ who appears as the one who ends the law; it is
this: does this book take its own peculiar hermeneutic disclosure
from the law or from Christ 'who ends the law' (Rom. 10.4)?
Christian faith understands the manifestation of Christ as the
decision of God; it will have understood the word which he had
spoken previously from the viewpoint of the good news of the
gospel that brings an end to the domination of the law.

It is not at all to the point to discern the great contrast and
deeply legal character of the Old Testament in its concern with
the world. This concern with the world proclaims quite un-
mistakably that God is at work in the world and will not leave it to
its self-contained closed system. The Old Testament is here an
excellent defence for the correct understanding of Christ, who is
not an event beyond the world but the presence of God's love
within the world. The Old Testament is the great interpreter of
this coming of God to the world which leaves no area to itself,
neither nature nor history, neither love nor power, neither state
nor the community of the pious. It allows Christ to be seen as king
with his claim on the world; the people of God receives a new
character from him and is opened up to the whole of the world.
God's royal will over every domain of man receives its fulfilment
in him.

The Church is always in danger of fashioning for herself a Christ who rules in a spiritual remoteness, and who experiences his true veneration in the church building or in theological discussions. But when the gospel of Christ is explained in terms of the Old Testament, then we see clearly that it is sent into the world, to the humble and to the suffering, as also to those in power and responsible for the laws of the state and of society; and so it becomes clear that God, the Lord and the creator of the whole world, will not be venerated in the world as the one who is beyond at an awesome distance, but will be loved again as the one who has come to the world in love.

NOTES

Introduction: The Old Testament and the World

[1] A. Harnack, *Das Evangelium vom fremden Gott* (1924).
[2] R. Bultmann, 'Prophecy and Fulfilment' in *Essays on Old Testament Interpretation*, ed. C. Westermann, EV ed. J. L. Mays: The Preacher's Library (1963), pp. 50–75.

CHAPTER 1
Israel and Her God

[1] For further details cf. W. Zimmerli, *The Law and the Prophets* (1965), pp. 9–11.
[2] See the important declaration in Exod. 19.5ff.
[3] O. Eissfeldt, *The Old Testament, An Introduction* (1966), pp. 169–70, includes a fourth strand, the 'lay-source', L. G. Fohrer (E. Sellin), *Introduction to the Old Testament* (1970), pp. 159–65, prefers the designation 'nomad-source', N.
[4] According to M. Noth, *A History of Pentateuchal Tradition* (1972), p. 36, this account is to be found in Exod. 3.4b; 6; 9–14(15).
[5] A. Alt, 'The God of the Fathers', in *Essays in Old Testament History and Religion* (1966), pp. 1–66.
[6] Does this indicate that the Yahwistic source originated in circles in which the Kenite tradition was alive? For the possibility of a pre-Mosaic worship of Yahweh in the Sinai peninsula, see S. Herrmann, 'Der alttestamentliche Gottesname', *Ev. Th.* 26 (1966), pp. 281–93, and *Israels Aufenthalt in Ägypten*, Stuttgarter Bibel-Studien, 40 (1970), especially pp. 41–3.
[7] For text, see J. B. Pritchard ed., *Ancient Near Eastern Texts* (ANET) (1955), pp. 376–8, and *The Ancient Near East in Pictures* (ANEP) (1954) n. 342ff.
[8] M. Noth, *Das System der zwölf Stämme Israels*, BWANT 4, Folge 1 (1930).
[9] R. Knierim, 'Das erste Gebot', SAW 77 (1965), pp. 20–39.
[10] B. Albrektson, *History and the Gods* (1967).
[11] See W. Zimmerli's discussion of Bloch's view in *Man and His Hope in the Old Testament* (1971), pp. 151–65.
[12] G. von Rad, 'The Form-Critical Problem of the Hexateuch', in *The*

Problem of the Hexateuch and Other Essays (1966), pp. 1–78.

[13] L. Rost, *Das kleine Credo und andere Studien zum Alten Testament* (1965), pp. 11–25.

[14] See the 'popular lament' in Jeremiah 14.19–22 which has been taken up into the 'Liturgy in time of drought' (Jer. 14.1—15.4).

[15] V. Maag has once more drawn particular attention to this in 'Das Gottesverständnis des Alten Testaments', *Ned. Th. T.* 21 (1966/67), pp. 161–207, with the literature referred to.

[16] 1 Sam. 9.16; 10.1 (LXX); 2 Sam. 3.18.

[17] In Isaiah 10.5 the attack is directed at the same time to the instrument of Yahweh's judgement which is comporting itself with such arrogance.

[18] Jer. 25.9; 27.6; 43.10. This shocking description of Nebuchadnezzar is better understood as belonging to a separate branch of the tradition rather than as the subsequent insertion of an honorific title.

[19] Isa. 45.1.

[20] W. Zimmerli, 'Der "neue Exodus" in der Verkundigung der beiden grossen Exilspropheten' in *Maqqêl shâqêdh. La Branche d'amandier*. Hommage à Wilhelm Vischer (1960), pp. 216–27 (= *Gottes Offenbarung. Gesammelte Aufzätze.* 2. Aufl. (1969), pp. 192–204).

CHAPTER 2
The World as God's Creation

[1] H. Gese, 'Die Religionen Altsyriens' in *Religionen Altsyriens, Altarabiens und der Mandäer. Religionen der Menschheit* 10, 2 (1970), pp. 1–232.

[2] W. Zimmerli, 'Abraham und Melchisedek' in *Das ferne und das nahe Wort.* Festschrift L. Rost, BZAW 105 (1967), pp. 255–64.

[3] C. Westermann, *Genesis*, Bk 1, 1966, pp. 270ff. has attempted to explain the quite striking double name 'Yahweh Elohim' which is used throughout Genesis 2.4b—3.24.

[4] If the Yahwist had resumed Kenite traditions (cf. ch. 1, n. 6), then it would not be at all impossible that the tradition of the beginnings could have its origin in the period before the taking of the land.

[5] Sanchuniaton's account, handed on by Eusebius, *Praeparatio Evangelica*, 1; 10, 1ff. is given both in the original text and in translation by O. Eissfeldt, *Taautos und Sanchunjaton*, SAB, K1. Sprachen (1952) 1, pp. 37ff.

[6] The word *'ōlām* in Qoheleth 3.11 should not be translated by 'world'. Cf. E. Jenni, 'Das Wort *'ōlām* im Alten Testament', ZAW 64 (1952), pp. 197–248; 65 (1953), pp. 1–35; also ATD 16, (1967)[2], pp. 172ff.

[7] Plato, *Timaeus* 92C: Loeb Classical Library.

[8] Kittel, *Theological Dictionary of the New Testament*, 1, 3, 874f., (1965).

[9] See Hebrew text in BHK[3].

[10] ANET: Princeton University Press (1955), pp. 60–72.

[11] ANET, pp. 99–100.

[12] Cf. Westermann, n. 3, pp. 36ff.

[13] So in the myth of Enki and Ninhursag, S. N. Kramer, *Sumerian Mythology* (1944), p. 57; for the Phoenician mythology, see n. 5.

[14] ANEP, n. 569.

[15] H. Kees, *Ägypten*, RGL², (1928), p. 2.

[16] K. Koch, 'Wort und Einheit des Schöpfergottes in Memphis und Jerusalem', ZTHK 62 (1965), pp. 251–93.

[17] It should be stated once more that this is a quite different matter from the confession of Yahweh who led them out of the land of Egypt.

[18] H. Kees, n. 15.

[19] According to Baumgartner, *Hebräisches und Aramaisches Lexikon zum Alten Testament* (1967),³ pp. 146–7, the old south Arabic *br'*, 'build', Soqotrian 'to bring forth', may be alleged for purposes of comparison. Baumgartner notes under *bārā'* 111, an independent root. It is used in the Old Testament in the Piel meaning 'cut down', 'root out'. In the basic form it should mean 'cut out', 'cut'.

[20] It is only in introducing the creation of man that the divine word of creation has not the form of a simple command.

[21] Gen. 1.4, 10, 12, 18, 21, 25. It is not clear why the phrase does not occur in 1.7.

[22] Gen. 1.31.

[23] E. Bloch, *Das Prinzip Hoffnung*, Gesamtausgabe Bd. 5 (1959), p. 855.

[24] The narrative moves from disobedience to the lord of Paradise in Genesis 3 to the murder of a brother and to the song of vengeance unlimited in Genesis 4; then to the obliteration of the boundaries between the divine and the human in the highly coloured mythological fragment of 6.1–4; to the unfilial contempt of a father in the story of the origin of the Canaanites in 9.18–27; and finally to the pride of the builders of the tower of Babel in 11.1–9.

[25] Gen. 11.1–9.

[26] T. Rendtorff and H. E. Tödt, *Theologie der Revolution. Analysen und Materialien* (1969),² p. 98.

CHAPTER 3
Be Fruitful and Increase, and Fill the Earth

[1] G. Wehmeier, *Der Segen im Alten Testament*, Diss. Basel (1970); C. Westermann, *Der Segen in der Bibel und im Handeln der Kirche* (1968).

[2] J. Hempel, 'Die israelitischen Anschauungen von Segen und Fluch im Lichte altorientalischer Parallelen' in ZDMG 79 (1925), pp. 20–110 (= *Apoxysmata*, BZAW 81 (1961), pp. 30–113.

[3] The versions suggest a slight variation.

[4] Professor Zimmerli cites the translation of the Zürich Bible; the NEB version is used here.

[5] Cf. ch. 4.

[6] Lev. 15; Deut. 13.11ff., etc.

[7] e.g. Exod. 19.15; 1 Sam. 21.5ff.

[8] Lev. 21.13ff.

[9] Judges 13.3–5; 7; 13ff. speaks of the restrictions imposed upon the mother of the Nazirite, and Judges 16.17 and Amos 2.11ff. of the restrictions prescribed for the Nazirite himself. Numbers 6 describes the regulations which govern one who has taken the Nazirite vow for a specified time.

[10] Jer. 35.6–10.

[11] Hos. 3.3. See Hebrew text in BHK.[3]

[12] Though they sound alike, the Hebrew words *'ish*, 'man', and *'ishshah*, 'woman', derive from different roots.

[13] G. Gerleman, *Das Hohelied*, BK XVIII 2. Teil (1965), pp. 60–62.

[14] Zimmerli uses Gerleman's version in the German text.

[15] Cf. Gerlemann, pp. 43–51.

[16] Cf. Gerlemann, p. 84.

[17] K. Elliger, 'Das Gesetz Leviticus 18', ZAW 67 (1955), pp. 1–25 (= *Kleine Schriften* (1966), pp. 232–59); *Leviticus*, HAT 4 (1966), ad loc.

[18] 2 Sam. 13.12.

[19] Gen. 34.7; Deut. 22.21; Judg. 20.6, 10; Jer. 29.23.

[20] Judges 19 gives an account of a similar perversion in Gibeah of the tribe of Benjamin.

[21] Exod. 20.14; Deut. 5.18.

[22] This is the presupposition in all three variants of the story of 'the ancestress in danger' (Gen. 12.10–20; 20.1–18; 26.7–11).

[23] G. Boström, 'Proverbiastudien', LUÅ FN. Avd. 1, Bd. 30, Nr. 3 (1935), pp. 120ff.

[24] 2 Sam. 13.

[25] W. Zimmerli, *Man and His Hope in the Old Testament* (1971), ch. 1.

[26] See commentary on text in W. Zimmerli, *Ezechiel*, BK XIII.

[27] See also the images in the prophetic declarations (Isa. 49.18; 61.10; 62.5).

CHAPTER 4
. . . And Subdue It

[1] H. Wildberger, 'Das Abbild Gottes', *ThZ* 21 (1965), pp. 245–59, 481–501. C. Westermann has dealt in detail with the history of the exegesis of Genesis 1.26ff. in *Genesis*, Bk 1 (1966), pp. 203–14.

[2] The word *elohim* has a different meaning here from that which it has in the priestly creation narrative. It does not signify God in his uniqueness and for this reason Yahweh is used in the verses that frame the Psalm. *Elohim* refers here to beings which surround the divinity and is rendered in the Greek versions by *angeloi*, which corresponds exactly with the sense intended.

[3] See Hebrew text in BHK[3].

[4] This command given to Noah (cf. further Lev. 17.10–16) was retained in Judaism in the ritual killing of animals and according to Acts 15 was still a matter of concern for the early Christians.

[5] G. von Rad, *Wisdom in Israel* (1972).

[6] H. H. Schmid, *Wesen und Geschichte der Weisheit: Eine Untersuchung zur altorientalischen und israelitischen Weisheits literatur*, BZAW 101 (1966). Further literature will be found here together with an examination of the wisdom of the world in which Israel lived.

⁷ W. Zimmerli, 'Die Weisung des Alten Testaments zum Geschäft der Sprache' in *Das Problem der Sprache in Theologie und Kirche*, herg. von W. Schneemelcher (1959), pp. 1–20 (= *Gesammelte Aufzätze*, 2. Aufl. (1969), pp. 277–99).

⁸ A. Alt first drew attention to the relationship of the Onomastika to Old Testament wisdom in his essay 'Die Weisheit Salomos', *ThLZ* 76 (1951), pp. 139–44 (= *Kleine Schriften zur Geschichte des Volkes Israel 11* (1953), pp. 90–99).

⁹ Alt, p. 95.

¹⁰ Alt, p. 94.

¹¹ Alt had already referred to this and von Rad has studied the question further in 'Hiob 38 und die altagyptische Weisheit', Supp VT 3 (1953), pp. 293–301.

¹² S. Herrmann, 'Die Naturlehre des Schöpfungberichtes. Erwägungen zur Vorgeschichte von Genesis 1', *ThLZ* 86 (1961), pp. 413–24.

¹³ The translation of verse 31 is uncertain.

¹⁴ H. Gese, *Lehre und Wirklichkeit in der alten Weisheit* (1958).

¹⁵ C. Kayatz, *Studien zu Proverbien 1–9*, WMANT 22 (1966).

¹⁶ Kayatz, p. 98.

¹⁷ K. Koch, 'Gibt es ein Vergeltungsdogma im Alten Testament?', *ZThK* 52 (1955), pp. 1–42.

¹⁸ For a discussion of the translation, see G. von Rad, *Wisdom in Israel* (1972), pp. 66–8.

¹⁹ In the following quotations in the German text, Zimmerli makes use of his translation in *Prediger*, ATD 16, 2. Aufl. (1967), pp. 123–253.

CHAPTER 5
The People and Its Enemies

¹ According to M. Noth, *Exodus* (1962), p. 138, the place name, Rephidim, has been added to this Yahwistic narrative from the priestly date of 17:1abi.

² For this translation and further commentary, see Noth's discussion.

³ M. Noth, *The History of Israel* (1960)², pp. 74 and 95 n. 3; *Das Buch Josua*, HAT , 7, 2. Aufl. (1953), pp. 20ff. Also K. Kenyon, *Digging up Jericho* (1957), pp. 256–65.

⁴ Noth, *The History of Israel*.

⁵ A. Alt, *Die Landnahme der Israeliten in Palästina*, *Reformationsprogramm der Universität Leipzig 1925*. (= *Kleine Schriften zur Geschichte des Volkes Israel 1* (1953), pp. 89–125); 'Erwägungen über die Landnahme der Israeliten in Palästina, PJ 35 (1939), pp. 8–73 (= *Kleine Schriften 1*, pp. 126–75).

⁶ A. Alt, 'Meros', ZAW 58 (1940/41), pp. 244–7 (= *Kleine Schriften 1*, pp. 274–7.

⁷ G. von Rad, *Der Heilige Krieg im alten Israel*, ATANT 20 (1951); R. Smend, *Yahwekrieg und Stämmebund*, FRLANT 84 (1963).

⁸ There is also mention of the 'wars of Yahweh' in 1 Samuel 18.17; 25.28.

⁹ The mention of Samuel in this verse of the Hebrew is a secondary addition.

[10] The word can also describe the liturgical praise of Yahweh. P. Humbert has already recognized it as describing a ritual shout, *La 'terou 'a'. Analyse d'un rite biblique* (1946).

[11] For this history of the ark see especially L. Rost, *Die Uberlieferung von der Thronnachfolge Davids*, BWANT 3, Folge 6 (1926), pp. 4–47; J. Maier, *Das Altisraelitische Ladeheiligtum*, BZAW 93 (1965).

[12] The text of this verse is somewhat uncertain.

[13] R. Frey, *Amos und Jesaja*, WMANT 12 (1963).

[14] J. Begrich, *Der syrisch-ephraimitsche Krieg und seine weltpolitischen Zusammenhänge*, ZDMG 83 (1929), pp. 213–37 (= *Gesammelte Studien zum Alten Testament* (1964), pp. 99–120; H. Donner, 'Israel unter den Völkern. Die Stellung der klassichen Propheten des 8. Jahrhunderts v. Chr. zur Aussenpolitik der Könige von Israel und Juda', Supp VT 11 (1964).

[15] E. Würthwein, 'Jes 7.1–9' in *Theologie als Glaubenswagnis*. Festschrift zum 80. Geburtstag von Karl Heim (1954), pp. 47–63 (= *Wort und Existenz. Studien zum Alten Testament* (1970), pp. 127–43.

[16] For Israel's use of language, cf. W. Zimmerli, 'Verkündigung und Sprache Jesjais', in *Fides et Communicatio*, Festschrift für M. Doerne (1970), pp. 441–54.

[17] Christ used almost the same words when rejecting the tempter (Matt. 4.7; Luke 4.12); the difference is that Ahaz is acting in disobedience.

[18] There is allusion to the events of 1 Kings 12 from the viewpoint of Judah.

[19] For this type of literary speech, cf. W. Zimmerli, 'Das Wort des göttlichen Selbsterweises (Erweiswort), eine prophetische Gattung' in *Mélanges bibliques rédigés en l'honneur de André Robert* (1957), pp. 154–64 (= *Gottes Offenbarung*, 2. Aufl. (1969), pp. 120–32).

[20] Cf. Exod. 23.4ff.; Deut. 22.1–4.

CHAPTER 6
Land and Possession

[1] M. Buber, *Israel und Palästina. Zur Geschichte einer Idee* (1950), pp. 149ff.

[2] S. Herrmann in his study *Die prophetischen Heilserwartungen im Alten Testament. Ursprung und Gestaltwandel*, BWANT 5, Folge 5 (1965), has dealt with the different formulations of the promise of the land as a basis of the prophetic promises also.

[3] The word 'God' occurs only in verse 6 of Genesis 23 where the dwellers in the land refer to Abraham as a 'prince of God', *n^e si 'elohim*. RSV has 'a mighty prince'.

[4] See Tolstoy's story, 'How much land does man need?'

[5] D. Daube, *Studies in Biblical Law* (1947), pp. 34ff.

[6] In the *Genesis-Apocryphon* from Qumran, 21.8–22, Abraham not only casts his eyes over the promised land, but also walks its length and breadth in accordance with the direction of Genesis 13.17. Cf. the commentary of J. A. Fitzmyer, *The Genesis Apocryphon of Qumran Cave 1* (1966); also A. Dupont-Sommer, *The Essene Writings from Qumran* (1961), pp. 289–91.

[7] Jer. 3.19.

[8] Dan. 8.9; 11.16, 41.

[9] For a detailed classification and distinction of the terms used for the land, cf. G. von Rad, 'The Promised Land and Yahweh's Land in the Hexateuch' in *The Problem of the Hexateuch and other Essays* (1966), pp. 79–93. H. Wildberger, 'Israel und sein land, *Ev. Th.* 16(1956), pp. 404–22; J. J. Stamm, *Der Staat Israel und die Landverheissungen der Bibel* (1961)².

[10] Cf. Num. 13.23, and the fruits brought back by those sent to spy out the land.

[11] A. H. J. Gunneweg, *Leviten und Priester. Hauptlinien der Traditionsbildung und Geschichte des israelitisch-jüdischen Kultpersonals*, FRLANT 89 (1965).

[12] P. Humber, 'Osée le prophète bédouin', *RHPhR* 1 (1921), pp. 97–118; 'La Logique de la perspective nomade chez Osée et l'unité d'Osée 2.4–22', BZAW 41, pp. 158–66. For Hosea and pertinent literature, cf. H. W. Wolff, *Dodekapropeton 1, Hosea*, BK xiv/1 (1961).

[13] A. Alt, 'Josua' in *Werden und Wesen des Alten Testaments*, BZAW 66 (1936), pp. 13–39 (= *Kleine Schriften 1* (1953), bes. 189–91).

[14] A. Alt, 'Micha 2, 1–5 GES ANADASMOS in Juda' in *Interpretationes ad Vetus Testamentum pertinentes Sigmundo Mowinckel septuagenario missae* (1955), pp. 13–23 (= *Kleine Schriften 111* (1959) pp. 373–81).

[15] Alt, p. 374, n. 14.

[16] W. Zimmerli, '*Planungen für den Wiederaufbau nach der Katastrophe von 587*' VT 19 (1969), pp. 229–55, bes. 246–50; *Ezechiel*, BK XIII (1969), pp. 1,202–35.

[17] G. Ch. Macholz, 'Noch Einmal: Planungen für die Wiederaufbau nach der Katastrophe von 587', VT 19 (1969), pp. 332–52.

[18] For the general structure and exegesis of Leviticus 25, see K. Elliger, *Leviticus*, HAR 1, 4 (1966), pp. 335–60.

[19] This, and not an arrangement for liturgical worship, is the primary meaning of the sabbath.

[20] Code of Hammurabi, n. 117, ANET, pp. 170ff.

[21] F. Horst, 'Das Eigentum nach dem Alten Testament', *Kirche im Volk Heft 2: Das Eigentum als Problem evangelischer Sozialethik* (1947), pp. 87–102 (= *Gottes Recht. Studien zum Recht im Alten Testament* (1961), p. 214).

[22] As in Gen. 12.6; 13.7.

[23] The parallel passage in Deuteronomy 5.21 leads the verb *hamad* in the direction of internal desire by using the verb '*iwwah*, whose original meaning is just this.

[24] J. Herrmann, 'Das zehnte Gebot' *Sellin-Festschrift* (1927), pp. 69–82.

CHAPTER 7
The People of Yahweh and the Worship of Yahweh

[1] M. Weber, *Gesammelte Aufsätze zur Religionssoziologie III. Das antike Judemtum* (1923)².

[2] Cf. n. 1, ch. 3, n. 18ff.

[3] The Yahwist includes the Mesopotamian world with them.

[4] The peoples of Mespotamia of course drop out of the Yahwist's list.

[5] For the world picture that lies behind this classification, cf. G. Hölscher, *Drei Erdkarten, Ein Beitrag zur Erkenntnis des hebräischen Altertums*, SAH Phil-Hist. Klasse Jahrgang (1944/48), 3 (1949).

[6] H. W. Wolff, *Dodekapropheton 2, Amos*, BK XIV/2, p. 399.

[7] 2 Sam. 15.18; 20.23.

[8] Ishmael, Gen. 16; 21; 25.12–18. Edom-Esau, Gen. 25.19–34; 27; 36. Moab and Ammon, Gen. 19.30–38.

[9] For discussion of the text, see BK XIII, 331ff.

[10] The Greek and Latin versions have preserved the original text. The Hebrew text has been altered for dogmatic reasons so as to avoid expressions that have echoes of polytheism. Instead of 'sons of God', *bᵉnē'el*, it reads 'sons of Israel', *bᵉnē' yisrā'el*.

[11] W. Zimmerli, 'Abraham und Melchisedek' in *Das ferne und nahe Wort*. Festschrift L. Rost, BZAW 105 (1967), pp. 255–67.

[12] Cf. n. 9.

[13] In the introductions, e.g. Rom. 1.7; 1 Cor. 1.2; 2 Cor. 1.1.

[14] A. Klostermann, 'Beiträge zur Entstehungsgeschichte des Pentateuchs', *ZLThK* 38 (1877), pp. 401–45 (= 'Ezechiel und das Heiligheitsgesetz' in *Der Pentateuch* (1893), pp. 368–418.

[15] Cf. n.9.

[16] Cf. ch. 1, n. 20.

CHAPTER 8
The People, the Neighbour, and Their Life before Yahweh

[1] A. Jepsen, 'Untersuchungen zum Bundesbuch', BWABT 3, Folge 5 (1927), pp. 55–81, speaks of 'Hebrew mishpatim'. A. Alt, 'The Origins of Israelite Law' in *Essays on Old Testament History and Religion* (1966), pp. 1–66, speaks of 'casuistic law'.

[2] A. Alt.

[3] ANET, p. 422.

[4] Cf. ch. 6, pp. 68–9.

[5] It has been very popular in recent times to bring the Decalogue down into the Deuteronomic period. The remarks in the book of Hosea forbid this.

[6] J. Hejcl, *Das Alttestamentliche Zinsverbot*, BSt, 12, 4 (1907).

[7] A. Bertholet, *Die Stellung der Israeliten und der Juden zu den Fremden* (1896); R. de Vaux, *Ancient Israel* (1961), pp. 74–6.

[8] G. von Rad, *Das Gottesvolk im Deuteronomium*, BWANT, 3, Folge 11 (1929) p. 9.

[9] Cf. ch. 6, p. 76.

[10] W. Zimmerli, 'Ich bin Jahwe' in *Geschichte und Altes Testament*. Festschrift für A. Alt (1953), pp. 179–209 (= *Gottes Offenbarung* (1969)², pp. 11–40); K. Elliger, 'Ich bin der Herr—euer God' in *Theologie als Glaubenswagnis*. Festschrift Karl Heim (1954), pp. 9–54 (= *Kleine Schriften zum Alten Testament* (1966), pp. 211–31).

[11] H. J. Kraus, *Worship in Israel* (1966).

[12] J. Begrich, *Die Chronologie der Könige von Israel und Juda*, BHTh 3 (1929), pp. 66–90. A change in the calendar in the year 605 under Jehoiakim, as accepted by K. S. Freedy and D. B. Redford, 'The Dates in Ezekiel in Relation to Biblical, Babylonian and Egyptian Sources', JAOS 90 (1970), pp. 462–85, seems to me from general historical considerations much less probable than the change accepted by Begrich in the time of Ahaz.

[13] L. Rost, 'Wiederwechsel und alttestamentlicher Festkalender', ZDPV 66 (1943), pp. 205–15 (= *Das kleine Credo und andere Studien zum Alten Testament* (1965), pp. 101–12.

[14] Exod. 12.29.

[15] Gen. 24.18; Exod. 24.4; Josh. 24.26.

[16] H. J. Hermisson has demonstrated convincingly in *Sprache und Ritus im alttestamentlichen Kult*, WMANT 19 (1965), that a spiritualizing application of cult concepts (e.g. circumcision, thanksgiving, sacrifice, etc.) is not to be interpreted as a polemic against the proper performance of the liturgy.

[17] For the different types of sacrifice, cf. R. Rendtorff, *Studien zur Geschichte des Opfers im Alten Israel*, WMANT 24 (1967).

CHAPTER 9
Death and Life

[1] H. W. Robinson, 'The Hebrew Conception of Corporate Personality', in *Werden und Wesen des Alten Testaments*, BZAW 66 (1936), pp. 49–62.

[2] Cf. ch. 1, p. 10

[3] Cf. ch. 7, p. 85

[4] G. von Rad, ' "Righteousness" and "Life" in the Cultic Language of the Psalms', in *The Problem of the Hexateuch and other Essays* (1966), pp. 243–66.

[5] J. Begrich, 'Die priesterliche Tora', in *Werden und Wesen des Alten Testaments*, BZAW 66 (1936), pp. 63–88 (= *Gesammelte Studien* (1964), pp. 232–60).

[6] See the judgement of E. Hirsch, *Das Alte Testament und die Predigt des Evangeliums* (1936); also F. Baumgärtel, *Verheissung. Zur Frage des evangslichen Verständnisses des Alten Testaments* (1952).

[7] See the literature in L. Wächter, 'Der Tod im Alten Testament', *Arbeiten zur Theologie* 11, 8 (1967), p. 181 Anm. 1.

[8] Ch. 6, p. 69.

[9] ANET, pp. 97–9; A. Schott and W. von Soden, *Das Gilgamesh-Epos*, Reclam-Bibliothek 7235/35a (1970).

[10] See Hebrew text in BHK³.

[11] A similar macabre note runs through the description in the Gilgamesh epic, cf. n. 9.

[12] For commentary on the text, see W. Zimmerli, *Ezechiel*, BK XIII (1959), pp. 773–93.

[13] AOB², n. 205.

[14] H. Bonnet, *Reallexikon der ägyptischen Religionsgeschichte* (1952), pp. 568–76; S. Morenz, ' Ägyptische Religion', *Die Religionen der Menscheit*, Band 8 (1960), under 'Osiris'; H. Gressmann, *Tod und Auferstehung des Osiris nach Festbräuchen und Umzügen*, AO 23, 3 (1923).

[15] W. Zimmerli, *Ezechiel*, pp. 218–20.

[16] According to H. Wildberger, *Jesaja*, BK x (1965), p. 71, the word *'Elim* echoes the idea of 'trees of God'.

[17] For this interpretation of *hamad*, cf. Wildberger, loc. cit., n. 16.

[18] W. Graf Baudissin, *Adonis und Esmun. Eine Untersuchung zur Geschichte des Glaubens an Auferstehungsgötter und an Heilgötter* (1911).

[19] German translation, C. Clemen, *Lukians Schrift über die syrische Göttin*, AO 37, 3/4 (1938).

[20] C. Bath, *Die Erettung vom Tode in den individuellen Klage- und Dankliedern des Alten Testaments* (1947).

[21] Should the text of verse 17 perhaps be emended to read 'ill' instead of 'fools'?

[22] H. Gunkel and J. Begrich, *Einleitung in die Psalmen*, HK 11, Ergänzungs-band (1933) pp. 408 ff.

[23] W. Zimmerli, ' "Leben" und "Tod" im Buche des Propheten Ezechiel', ThZ 13 (1957), pp. 494–508 (= *Gottes Offenbarung* (1969)², pp. 178–191).

[24] R. Rentdorff, *Die Gesetze in Der Priesterschrift*, FRLANT 62 (1954), pp. 74–6; G. von Rad, 'Faith Reckoned as Righteousness', in *The Problem of the Hexateuch and Other Essays* (1966), pp. 125–30.

[25] Cf. G. von Rad (n. 24).

CHAPTER 10
The Hope of Israel and the Hope of the World

[1] 2 Sam. 7. See M. Noth, 'David und Israel in 2 Sam. 7', in *Mélanges bibliques rédigés en l'honneur de André Robert* (1957), pp. 122–30 (= *Gesammelte Studien zum Alten Testament* (1960)², pp. 334–45; for another view, see H. Gese, 'Der Davidbund und die Zionserwählung', ZThK 61 (1964), pp. 10–26.

[2] A. R. Johnson, *Sacral Kingship in Ancient Israel* (1955); even more critical, K. H. Bernhardt, 'Das Problem der altorientalischen Königsideologie im Alten Testament', Supp VT 8 (1961).

[3] G. von Rad, 'The Royal Ritual in Judah', in *The Problem of the Hexateuch and Other Essays* (1966), pp. 222–31.

[4] G. von Rad, *Studies in Deuteronomy* (1953).

[5] H. W. Wolff, *Dodekapropheton* 2 BK XIV/2 (1969), pp. 403ff.

[6] A. Alt, 'Jes 8, 23–9, 6. Befreiungsnacht und Krönungstag' in Festschrift A. Bertholet (1950), pp. 29–49 (= *Kleine Schriften 11* (1953), pp. 206–25; H. Wildberger, *Jesaja* BK x (1970), pp. 362–89.

[7] For text and interpretation, see W. Zimmerli, *Ezechiel*, BK XIII (1069), pp. 825–49.

[8] See Hebrew text, BHK³.

[9] Matt. 9.27; 15.22; 20.30ff; Mark 10.47ff; Luke 18.38ff.

[10] H. D. Preuss, *Yahweglaube und Zukunftzerwartung*, BWABT 5, Folge 7 (1968), approaches the question from the structure of the Exodus Credo. See also W. Zimmerli, *Man and His Hope in the Old Testament* (1971).

[11] Ezekiel 20.40 speaks of the high mountain of Israel.

[12] See Hebrew text, BHK³.

[13] See Hebrew text, BHK³.

[14] For a survey of the state of the question to 1963, see C. R. North, *The Suffering Servant in Deutero-Isaiah* (1963)².

[15] For the relationship between prophecy and apocalyptic, see P. von der Osten-Sacken, *Die Apokalyptik in ihrem Verhältnis zu Prophetie und Weisheit*, ThEx 157 (1969).

[16] *Ezechiel*, BK XII (1969), pp. 921–75.

[17] H. W. Wolff, *Dodekapropheton 2*, BK XIV/2 (1969).

[18] R. Hanhart, 'Die Heiligen des Höchsten' in *Hebräische Wortforshung*, Festschrift W. Baumgartner, Supp VT 16 (1967), pp. 90–101.

[19] The interpretation of this half-verse is uncertain.

[20] The Greek tradition is preferred here to the MT.

[21] Gen. 5.24; 2 Kings 2.10.

[22] See F. Horst, *Hiob*, BK XVI (1968), p. 278. Zimmerli follows Horst in the German text.

CHAPTER 11
The Old Testament and the World: Law or Gospel

[1] In the German text Zimmerli follows the pagination of Bultmann's essay as it appears in *Glauben und Verstehen 11* (1952), pp. 162–86. The pagination here follows that of the English version as given at the beginning of the text of ch. 11.

[2] p. 63.

[3] p. 67.

[4] p. 68.

[5] p. 69.

[6] pp. 71–2.

[7] p. 73.

[8] p. 73.

[9] p. 74.

[10] p. 75.

[11] This is a quotation from another essay in *Glauben und Verstehen 11*, 'Das Verständnis von Welt und Mensch im Neuen Testament und im Griechentum', 59–78 (p. 73), which first appeared in ThBl 19 (1940), pp. 1–14. This essay is equally important for the problem under consideration.

[12] 1 John 16.33.

[13] 1 John 5.4.

[14] Cf. ch. 7 and the discussion there of the 'glory' of Israel.

[15] T. C. Vriezen has suggested the description 'actual-eschatological', in 'Prophecy and Eschatology', Supp VT 1 (1953), pp. 199–29 (p. 225).

[16] The purpose of the series of lectures in the books, *The Law and the Prophets* (1965), was to demonstrate this.

INDEX OF NAMES AND SUBJECTS

INDEX OF SCRIPTURE REFERENCES